Praise for *Informal Le*

"Paul has clearly identified where informal le. ⌐ ┌ ⌐ ┌ ⌐ ┌ ⌐ ─ ┌ ⌐ and high impact ways of improving workforce engagement and capability."

David Apparicio

Former Head of Learning & Development, The Royal Mail

"In order to meet the challenge of equipping a public service organisation to develop and improve on performance in today's climate, something new is required. 'Informal Learning' has changed my mindset and provided a framework and direction for how that can be better achieved."

Adrian Kingswell

Head of Learning & Development, Hampshire Constabulary

"Hurrah!! Finally, a book that doesn't just theorise about informal learning, but actually provides real-world, practical advice for making it happen. In the current climate of over-stretched L&D resources and budget, this book really does open the door to creating a true learning culture by harnessing what our employees do naturally. By applying the advice in this book, enhanced employee engagement and increased organisational performance will inevitably follow."

Nicki Talbot

Director – Learning & Development, Colt Technology

"Too few business leaders recognise the importance of informal learning in the development of their people and hence the value such learning can contribute to the future prosperity of their enterprise. 'Informal Learning at Work' provides a very readable explanation of the value to be derived from this aspect of learning together with practical examples of how it works and why."

Andrew Hall

Group Chairman, Vistage UK

"A refreshing read that provides the L&D specialist with a clear mandate to immerse themselves in the business, work with leaders and managers and be a fundamental part of the learning process with people in their daily working activities. A helpful insight into placing learning as part of the change agenda and working with learners innate abilities to self-learn when it matters to them not when the training department tells them. Learners, leaders and managers will need to know how to do this, this is the new role for L & D – a paradigm shift for traditionalists."

Carol Bolton

Organisational Development Manager, University of Liverpool

"Informal learning drives competitive advantage; this book tells you how to harness informal learning in the workplace to drive engagement and workforce capability. It is a fantastic tool that enables employees to leverage their knowledge and share their skills whilst completing their daily activities, resulting in a low cost, but highly effective option for improving performance across the entire organisation."

Sarah Menday

Learning Solutions Manager, Home Retail Group

"At last, a thought provoking practical book with ideas and insightful examples which challenges us all to embrace informal learning. This book is an easy read, filled with wonderful stories and great ideas which invite us all to re think how we work within our organisations."

Christina Bush

Learning & Development Manager, large supermarket chain

"Paul sets out his case succinctly and manages to distil, in a very easy to read book, clarity, common sense and a way forward from the often over-crowded debate on the future direction of workplace learning."

Derek Brimley

Learning Manager, aviation industry

"Paul clearly explains the shift in expectations on L&D professionals these days and explores the new opportunities that are available without disregarding the value of traditional training routes should they still be applicable. A good read and I would recommend this to anyone joining our team to understand the relative benefits of formal and informal learning."

Fiona Jones

Senior Management Development Advisor, large financial institution

"A really practical book with plenty of examples and tools to encourage L&D professionals to become learnscapers. I love the helpful and engaging quotations that will motivate those involved in workplace learning to "seed, weed, feed and breed"

Linda Walker

Senior People and Learning Manager (West Scotland), British Red Cross

informal learning
Learning
AT WORK

PAUL MATTHEWS

informal
learning
AT WORK

HOW TO BOOST PERFORMANCE IN TOUGH TIMES

Three Faces Publishing

First published in 2013 by
Three Faces Publishing
Alchemy House
17 Faraday Drive
Milton Keynes
MK5 7DD
United Kingdom

www.threefacespublishing.com
info@threefacespublishing.com

British Library Cataloguing in Publication Data
A CIP catalogue record for this book is available from the British Library

ISBN 978-1-909552-00-5

The Publisher's policy is to use paper manufactured from sustainable forests.

Printed and bound in the UK by TJ International Ltd, Padstow, Cornwall

Typeset by Ramesh Kumar P.

Thank you

We rarely travel alone.

Many people have been involved with bringing this book into being; from people who were prepared to indulge me in endless conversations about the core ideas, to people like Marie-Louise Cook, Diana Lodge and Rachel Wolverson who had a much more hands on role in converting the ideas into a manuscript.

To one and all... a heartfelt thanks for helping me on my journey.

Paul

Contents

Foreword by Donald H. Taylor

The past decade has seen a transformation in the way we learn at work. The leisurely world where organizations trained to an annual schedule of classroom courses is gone. In its place are demands for a faster initial speed to competence, for performance support initiatives and for business-aligned skills development.

That's a big change.

One thing that has not changed, however, is the overall aim of training and learning. As always, it is the role of learning and development professionals to ensure their organizations have the skills to deliver on their promises, both now and in the future.

But if the aim remains the same, the ways in which we achieve that aim are now more diverse than ever, and with the proliferation of opportunities for learning in today's connected world, the training department is no longer at the controlling centre of all activity. It is no longer the sole provider of information and skills. It cannot be, in an era where information is widely available at almost no cost, and nor should it be. Instead, its role has changed to ensuring people have high-quality opportunities to learn – both from the right materials, and from each other.

We should regard this new, wider remit as liberation from the limiting 20th century view of how people learn. In particular the availability of near instant communication in the 21st century has brought informal learning to the fore. Largely ignored by the profession before Jay Cross published *Informal Learning* in 2006, this most natural way of learning has exploded in importance with today's near ubiquity of social networking and mobile internet access.

Paul Matthews' work takes us another step forward in our understanding and appreciation of informal learning, and does so in a very pragmatic way. This book does not claim that all learning should be informal, nor does it claim that informal learning will flourish organically without being nurtured. Importantly, it emphasises the role of managers in the adoption and use of informal learning, and stresses that performance improvement via informal learning is not only an end in its own right, but also a way of ensuring the active support of those managers.

The learning profession has a new role, very different from the 'stand and deliver' role of the past, and this book provides a valuable guide to an important part of that new role – informal learning.

By Donald H. Taylor, Chairman, Learning and Performance Institute

Foreword by David Apparicio

Low Cost, High Impact Learning – Informal Learning

I think we all recognise that the only real differences between one organization and another are the people within it. People are the true differentiator.

Many businesses spend thousands and sometimes millions to have:

- experts come in to review systems, processes and ways of working, and then recommend improvements
- a business solutions team to install a new total quality methodology
- the latest training programmes delivered to employees
- the newest and most efficient equipment, systems, production lines or technology.

And the problem is that any other business can do the same, resulting in a situation where competitors can always 'catch-up'. These things are not enough on their own. Something more is needed to build a truly unique and high performing business. The answer lies in the people and their ability to learn fast enough to keep pace with the changes happening around us.

Paul explores the Agile Learning Organization and its critical role in business sustainability and performance. He has clearly identified where informal learning can provide cost effective and high impact ways of improving workforce engagement and capability. He also explores barriers to learning, an often overlooked factor when people are developing learning strategies.

Most importantly of all though, is the recognition that informal learning is already taking place within your organization. You need to guide and direct it so your workforce can learn when and how they need to learn, resulting in better retention of learning. By applying some simple steps we can create a supported learning culture that enables informal learning to thrive and grow. This results in a more agile learning organization that flexibly responds to the ongoing learning needs of its entire workforce.

As Chairman of The British Institute for Learning & Development, I am delighted that this book has been written, and even more delighted that the contents are so practical.

David Apparicio, JP, FRSA, FBILD, LiCIPD, FITOL
Chairman of The British Institute for Learning & Development (www.thebild.org)
Former Head of Learning & Development at The Royal Mail

Chapter 1

Survive and thrive with informal learning

"I want to talk about learning. But not the lifeless, sterile, futile, quickly forgotten stuff that is crammed in to the mind of the poor helpless individual tied into his seat by ironclad bonds of conformity!

"I am talking about LEARNING – the insatiable curiosity that drives the adolescent boy to absorb everything he can see or hear or read about gasoline engines in order to improve the efficiency and speed of his 'cruiser'. I am talking about the student who says, 'I am discovering, drawing in from the outside, and making that which is drawn in a real part of me.'

"I am talking about any learning in which the experience of the learner progresses along this line: 'No, no, that's not what I want'; 'Wait! This is closer to what I am interested in, what I need'; 'Ah, here it is! Now I'm grasping and comprehending what I need and what I want to know!'"

Carl Ransom Rogers[1]

Phil was a forklift driver in an ice cream factory and spent his working hours skilfully manoeuvring pallets across the icy floors of the warehouse.

I think to Phil's mind it wasn't the most exciting of jobs, but, with his learning difficulty, he doubted he would ever qualify for something better.

I met Phil while I was working at the same ice cream factory to earn money to pay my way through university. In our breaks, we'd sit outside in the sunshine and chat. During those chats, I discovered that Phil had a phenomenal knowledge of famous historic battles. He could recount the causes and outcomes of many of history's great battles and explain the tactics and psychology of the men who'd led them – Alexander, Napoleon, Washington, Saladin, Lee and Grant...

In his spare time, Phil's hobby was wargaming. He and his friends would recreate famous battles using model soldiers.

Phil didn't just recite a list of battles – he knew so much about the context of each battle that he could bring each one to life. He could explain what caused the battle and the political fallout afterwards. When he told me about a battle, I felt as if the two of us were silent spectators, watching from the trees or nearby encampment as events unfurled. As he spoke, I could imagine the boom of cannons, the screams of the defeated and the smell of gunpowder on the air.

He was such a master storyteller that I came to dread the end of our break times when I would be unceremoniously dragged back from the past and left to continue my shift loading ice cream pallets inside the sub-zero warehouse.

In a rare moment when Phil seemed to have run out of steam, I asked him, "How did you learn all this stuff?"

He looked uncomfortable. "I didn't. I just picked it up as I went along."

I thought of Phil while I was writing this book and how what he said all those years ago was a pretty good definition of informal learning. It's not scheduled; it's spontaneous. It just happens.

It happens when we make a mistake. It happens when we observe others doing either well or badly. When we see someone walk across a wet road and step into a deep puddle, we register the information. When we need to cross the same road, we will give the puddle a wide berth. We noticed something, we remembered it, and we changed our behaviour as a result. That's an example of informal learning in action. Sometimes, as with Phil, or when observing the puddle, we are not even consciously aware that we have learnt something. This lack of awareness is intriguing, and I believe counts for a lot of the confusion around the concept of informal learning.

If I need to buy a new photocopier, I will look on the internet to find out what is available. I won't consider my online search involves 'learning'. I won't think, "I am now going to learn about photocopiers." Much of the learning we do on a daily basis is not something we think of or label as learning.

Informal learning happens when people chat about their experiences, or ask someone a question. It happens when they look up information using Google, or go to a specialized website. It happens when they pick up an old manual or handbook to check something.

Informal learning is ubiquitous: it happens everywhere all the time. It is like breathing: it's natural and we can't stop doing it any more than we can stop breathing. Much of it is simply a side-effect of living our lives.

In the workplace, informal learning can be self-directed learning: the learner sets the objectives and pulls the information they need. In that moment, they are highly motivated to find information and to use it. It can also happen without any self-direction, when someone is exposed to information they are not looking for, yet they absorb and remember it, and maybe later use it. The classic example of this is the overheard water cooler conversation.

With formal learning, by comparison, someone or something (usually the Learning and Development department) sets the goals and objective. The organization has an explicit goal (for example, it wants employees to learn to operate a new machine or master a skill set) and the process is formal (for example, employees are sent to learn about the machine or skill set in a classroom, with an instructor or manual). The information is pushed at them.

But research has revealed that people learn much more about their jobs informally – by asking questions of colleagues, chatting, observing, or looking for the information online or on the company's intranet – than they do formally (through an organized training programme, for example). They learn informally because their perceptions are open and attuned to any information that passes them by that is relevant to their job. They want to do their jobs more effectively and efficiently: to fill in the gaps left by training, to learn new skills the workplace demands, and to increase opportunities for advancement and self-satisfaction.

An Atos KPMG study found that 80 per cent of learning in the workplace is informal and 20 per cent is formal. Many other studies have come up with similar results.

Work by Morgan McCall, Robert W. Eichinger and Michael M. Lombardo at the Center for Creative Leadership led to the oft-quoted '70:20:10' concept, which posits that around 70 per cent of learning happens on the job, 20 per cent happens through interaction with others and only 10 per cent occurs as a result of formal learning. Incidentally, the 70:20:10 concept is just that: a concept, not a framework. More on that later...

Until very recently, informal learning was under the radar as far as Learning and Development (L&D) professionals were concerned. While university scholars were busy researching and arguing over definitions of informal learning, L&D professionals in organizations were focused on formal learning. Their efforts were primarily channelled into providing formal training programmes to meet the needs of their organization's employees.

This might have continued were it not for the tumultuous economic, technological and demographic changes that have taken place in the past decade or so. The continuing impact of these changes on organizations and their employees is, and probably will continue to be, profound.

Just recently, NASA landed its one-tonne Curiosity robot on Mars – an incredible achievement and one which will provide scientists around the world with much-needed data about one of the planets within our planetary system. A few years ago, however, NASA was facing a major problem – many of its most experienced scientists and engineers were nearing retirement age and the space agency didn't have adequate systems in place to retain most of what those people knew.[2] In other words, once those people retired, the knowledge they had accumulated over many missions and years would be lost. These were people who had worked on the Apollo mission to the moon and had built the first space shuttle. For an agency like NASA, they represented billions of dollars of investment.

Imagine for a moment what it would be like to lose that kind of knowledge in your organization and the implications it would have...

If your organization is like many others and you have many senior employees (baby boomers), this is about to happen, because many of those people are on the verge of retirement. The invaluable knowledge they have acquired over many years – formally and informally – will vanish the day of their retirement party.

That's just one of the challenges companies and institutions face today. There are plenty more…

Increased competition has meant there's been a reduction in discretionary time in the workforce. The result is that employees have less time for activities that aren't viewed as immediately productive. Since classroom training takes employees away from their current responsibilities, supervisors and senior managers are less supportive of training activities. In addition, the economic pressures have meant many companies have cut back on training budgets.

In organizations that are responding well to these changes, this has led to a shift in focus from training to learning. Training is a brief episode, whereas learning is ongoing, and the responsibility shifts towards the learner. This shift increases the relevance of what people learn, and the learner more readily identifies with it, in comparison to material presented to them on a training course. So what does this shift in emphasis mean in practice?

Companies recognize that they need to offer products and services that are perceived to deliver high value to their customers. This value will be created by the acquisition and then application of the knowledge and skills of the workforce. The more skilled and knowledgeable the workforce and, crucially, the more capable they are of applying what they know, the greater the value of products and services produced and the more profitable the organization.

How will employees become the agile, innovative high performers their organizations need? Probably not by attending costly training programmes, but by learning the way people most like to learn – informally – asking questions of colleagues, collaborating, listening, testing new ideas, job sharing, failing, observing, job shadowing, watching videos, sharing experiences in hallways and online via social networking sites, and reading articles and emails on mobile phones...

Although L&D can't manage or measure this kind of learning in the way they might be used to, what they can and must do is to enhance their organization's informal learning environment to make it easier for workers to access the information they want and need, and then to share it with others.

This offers a huge opportunity for L&D to step up to this new reality and expand their role within their organizations. The recent decimation of the L&D budget has not reduced the relevance or scope of L&D. If anything, it has simply accelerated a trend that had already started, and savvy L&D people are changing the way they do things to bring focus onto the real powerhouse of learning in any workplace – the informal learning environment.

When companies are able to provide learning in the way employees want, learner satisfaction and engagement increases. Engaged employees perform better and are more productive than those who are not. They are more motivated to use what they've learned to come up with improved ways of tackling organizational challenges.

One pathway to organizational success is informal learning, according to Jay Cross, one of its foremost proponents and author of *Informal Learning: Rediscovering the Natural Pathways That Inspire Innovation and Performance*, the book that really turned the spotlight on the subject for the L&D profession.[3]

"Executives don't want learning, they want execution," he says. "They want the job done. They want performance. Informal learning is a profit strategy."

Companies are already applying it to reap these benefits: increase sales by making product knowledge instantly searchable; improve knowledge worker productivity; transform an organization from near bankruptcy to record profits; generate fresh ideas and increase innovation; reduce stress, absenteeism, and health care costs; invest development resources where they will have the most impact; increase professionalism and professional growth, and cut costs and improve responsiveness with self-service learning.

To improve performance in an organization, L&D needs to embrace and enhance informal learning and this requires a radical shakeup of the L&D role, from that of training provider to learning enabler. Don't take workers out of the workplace to give them training; instead, put the opportunities to learn in the workplace, right where they are needed.

L&D departments must stop being passive providers of training and become strategic partners with the C-suite and other key stakeholders within the organization – employees, line managers, senior managers – and perhaps outside the organization (customers and suppliers, for example).

L&D professionals need to ensure that learning, training and development interventions reflect business priorities. When they do this, they will be respected and supported within the organization and gain important backing from senior management.

This book reveals the challenges L&D professionals face right now, thanks to the sea change that is taking place, and shows how those challenges paradoxically provide them with the opportunity to become so much more than training providers. It explains the new L&D role – and how L&D can contribute to meeting business challenges.

Performance is crucial to the survival and future success of any organization, large or small, but improvements will only happen if people throughout the organization are encouraged to learn faster and more efficiently, and to use and share what they learn with others.

This book provides examples of how informal learning is happening in organizations around the world – from small private to large public companies to government agencies, such as NASA and the Central Intelligence Agency (CIA).

More importantly, it gives you practical advice about where to start with informal learning: how to identify, support and enhance the informal learning networks that already exist in your company.

The key point is this: the challenges aren't going to go away. L&D people who stick rigidly to the traditional formal learning paths will suffer the consequences, but those who can take up the challenge and creatively support informal learning, integrating it into the company culture, will be the L&D success stories of the 21st century. There will always be the need for a certain amount of formal learning, more or less depending on the nature of your business, but the up and coming generation thrives on informal learning. Your job now is to make it work smoothly, guide it to ensure the right things are learned, turn your company into a learning culture and deliver what the C-suite wants.

The learning organization

Success today and in the future depends on an organization's ability to outperform its competitors and deliver high value products or services. Competition is ferocious and escalating – pricing and profit margins are under pressure. Only those that can keep ahead of their competitors in terms of improving and sustaining performance will survive.

To achieve that, they need employees who are highly motivated and able to learn, innovate and adapt to external changes that are taking place at breakneck speed.

In the words of Peter Senge, "In the long run, the only sustainable source of competitive advantage is your organization's ability to learn faster than its competition. No outside force can take the momentum of that advantage away from you."[4]

Continuous improvement is critical and companies need to be agile, flexible and able to learn faster and faster, just to maintain their market share. But learning is the beginning of a journey, not the ultimate destination. What is learned on the job needs to be put into practice. To be really effective, learning has to be transferred – to be used, shared and ongoing. Sustained learning leads to capability, and it is employee capability that is crucial.

Competitive advantage comes from making sense of the vast volume of information that is available, and then sharing that understanding. For information is not knowledge – it is just intelligible data. Knowledge results when someone uses information to produce something new, combining it with other information to produce new information or to acquire new skills.

As L&D expert Bob Mosh says, "We are in the performance business, not the knowledge-gain business. The learning leaders who understand the difference are the ones who succeed."[5]

The challenges L&D face

Given an organization's dependence on such a strategic capability, you would think that learning and development would be treated as an absolute priority by any organization that has success in its sights.

Yes, many organizations say that learning is their upmost priority, but studies show that's rarely the case. Learning and development is unfortunately more often regarded as a business cost, rather than a crucial investment in an organization's survival. Sometimes, it's even seen as a distraction instead of a critical factor in performance.

Senior executives often regard investment in training and development as an expense. Worse, they often see it as a wasted expense.

A study of 500 senior managers by Capita Learning & Development revealed that 70 per cent fear that the inadequate skills of their staff will hold them back as the UK emerges from the current economic downturn.[6] About 46 per cent of those business leaders cast doubt on their L&D department's ability to deliver the skills needed to help their organization grow.

Over half (55 per cent) claim their firm is failing to deliver the necessary training for recovery. Around half fear for their company's ability to respond to surges in demand (51 per cent), retrain and redeploy people where required (47 per cent), and identify where current skills are becoming obsolete (49 per cent).

Even more worryingly, workers are still struggling to catch up with the impact of the downturn. More than two thirds (67 per cent) of business leaders are concerned their employees are struggling to cope with expanded remits following job cuts.

The vast majority (82 per cent) of leaders lack confidence that their firm's L&D strategy and delivery is aligned to the company's operational strategy. Half (50 per cent) believe that their L&D function is stuck in a 'business as usual' mind-set.

A 2010 McKinsey Global Survey indicated that nearly 75 per cent of those questioned do not believe their companies are effective at building the capabilities they need (McKinsey defined capability as 'anything that an organization does well that drives meaningful business results').[7] In particular, it pointed to the failure of training programmes to build the capabilities they need.

Three-quarters of the nearly 1,500 senior managers at 50 organizations interviewed by the Corporate Leadership Council were dissatisfied with their company's L&D function. Only one in four reported that L&D was critical to achieving business outcomes.[8]

Fewer than one in four Chief Learning Officers surveyed by the Internet Time Alliance said their employees were learning fast enough to keep up with the needs of the business.[9]

Chris Sharp, Managing Director, Capita Learning & Development, commenting on the Capita study says, "The post-recession landscape demands a range of new skills. Yet the UK workforce is critically lacking essential capabilities.

"Firms have failed to provide the right training through turbulent times and arm their staff with the skills needed for recovery. There is a real risk that this will leave UK Plc. exposed when the upturn finally arrives.

"As companies now position for growth, L&D strategy needs to catch up fast and evolve in line with firms' recovery strategies."

This all sounds like a pretty dire indictment of the L&D profession. It certainly makes tough reading for L&D people (unless you are one of the good ones), but I remember someone telling me that if there are lots of fires burning, you can easily become a hero by putting out just a few of them. Within these challenges faced by L&D are the seeds of a new way forward. Clearly what has been done is no longer working so well. The question now is how L&D people can change what they are doing to bring learning within organizations up to where it needs to be so people can develop the skills they, and the organization, need.

Managers lack skills

It's not just non-management employees who lack skills. Their managers, who play a crucial role in employees' learning, lack leadership and management skills. Research in the UK and abroad has shown that, despite considerable investment in management training and development in both the public and private sectors, much of the skill base of managers remains unimproved, according to those who work for them.

Research from the Chartered Institute of Personnel and Development (CIPD)/ Cornerstone OnDemand shows the UK's eight million managers lack leadership and management skills, according to their employees.[10] In its quarterly 'Employee outlook' survey of 2,000 employees, the CIPD found that there was a significant contrast between how managers say they manage their people and the views of their employees.

Another survey, 'The lessons for leaders from the people who matter', conducted at the end of 2011 by talent management firm Development Dimensions International (DDI), found that leaders worldwide lack empathy with their staff, have poor leadership skills, and a third of them are ineffective. The report found one in three employees (34 per cent) only "sometimes" or "never" consider their leader to be effective, and over a third (37 per cent) are only "sometimes" or "never" motivated to give their best by their leader.[11]

The poll of more than 1,250 full-time employees in non-management positions in the US, UK, Australia, Canada, China, India, Germany and South East Asia (Malaysia, Philippines and Singapore), found that they would rather suffer a bad hangover, do housework or see their credit card bill arrive in the mail, than face the prospect of sitting through a performance discussion with their boss.

Far from inspiring people to perform at their best, it seems more than half the bosses damaged their employees' self-esteem at some point. Only 40 per cent of respondents reported that their boss "never" damaged their personal self-esteem, which means 60 per cent had managers who damaged their self-esteem "sometimes", "most of the time" or "all of the time".

A survey by Orion Partners found that 24 per cent of employees thought their bosses were overstressed, poor communicators and lacked empathy – a combination judged to be counterproductive and in some cases destructive by the report. Almost half (47 per cent) of the 2,000 workers surveyed said that their managers made them feel threatened rather than rewarded.[12]

The impact managers have in terms of employee motivation and productivity is significant, yet these findings show that they are not only failing in their obligation to employees and, therefore, their organization, they're actually having a negative impact on the self-confidence of the organization's employees.

"Managers consistently delude themselves about how much good they're doing," says Robert Sutton, Professor of Management Science and Engineering at Stanford University. "The oath for managers should be the same as for physicians: First do no harm."

Given the need for companies to have employees who are highly motivated to learn and to perform, the consequences of managers with poor leadership skills are enormous. It's highly unlikely employees with managers who consistently damage their self-esteem will be motivated to perform at a high level.

CLC Human Resources found in its research 'Managing in the Downturn: Four Imperatives to Drive Employee Innovation and Performance' that "managers are increasingly important for improving discretionary effort: the impact of manager quality on whether employees go above and beyond the call of duty has jumped by 50 per cent since the recession began. On the flip side, bad bosses sap motivation, kill productivity and drive everyone crazy".

Employees who are most committed perform 20 per cent better than those who are not and are 87 per cent less likely to leave the organization, indicating the significance of engagement to organizational performance, according to a Corporate Leadership Council survey of more than 50,000 employees at 59 global organizations.[13]

While employees' commitment to their manager is crucial to engagement, the manager is most important as the enabler of employees' commitment to their jobs, organizations and teams, the survey concluded.

Employee engagement is a prerequisite of high performance and, as these surveys and reports have shown, organizations are failing to provide environments that make this possible.

Too much focus on formal learning

Almost all organizations spend the majority of their learning budgets on formal learning interventions – interventions that have the least impact on employee knowledge, performance and productivity.[14]

Study after study has shown that employees only learn about 10 per cent of what they need to know on the job from formal learning experiences. The majority of their learning happens informally – through observation, conversation with colleagues, trial and error, and so on.

In a formal learning environment, the training or learning department sets the goals and objectives, and then pushes the information at the learner. Informal learning means the learner sets the goals and objectives, pulling the information as required at time of need.

The more control of learning resides with the learner, the more likely it is that the learning will be of an informal nature. That's not to say that informal learning cannot convert to formal learning, or that an individual worker has no personal authority to decide to take a formal course. Nevertheless, if the learner knows what they want to learn, chooses how, when and where to learn it, and then decides for themselves whether they have learnt it, this would fall within the definition of informal learning.[15]

Formal training is inadequate to develop all the practices necessary to operate and thrive in an ever more complex working world. We all know people who have returned from a training course only to slot back into the same behaviours that the training course was supposed to change. They can't do what is expected and required, so their managers say they need to be trained again because the training failed. If something isn't working well, surely it is time to find out why and consider doing things differently?

Jim Clemmer, author and organizational expert, says investment in training is often wasted.[16] "Most organizations use their training investments about as strategically as they deploy their office supplies spending. And the impact on customer satisfaction, cost containment or quality improvement is just as useless.

"One of the biggest causes of wasted training dollars is ineffective methods. Too often, companies rely on lectures ('spray and pray'), inspirational speeches or videos, discussion groups and simulation exercises."

Unfortunately, research has shown these methods rarely change behaviour on the job.

"Knowing isn't the same as doing; good intentions are too easily crushed by old habits," says Clemmer. "What happens in the classroom and what happens back on the job are often worlds apart. Trainees learn which hoops to jump through, pledge alliance to the current management fad, give their enthusiastic 'commitment' to building 'the new culture', get their diploma – and then go back to work."

And yet, training is still where L&D invest their budget and hopes. The CIPD says, in its Learning and Talent Development Survey 2012, that although traditional methods of workplace learning are considered amongst the least effective ways to upskill employees, they still dominate the majority of learning and development programmes.

When asked to choose the most effective ways of delivering training, 16 per cent of learning and talent development professionals opted for formal education courses, and the same number for coaching by external practitioners. Only 11 per cent pointed to e-learning. But despite doubts about its effectiveness, less than a fifth (17 per cent) of the report's respondents plan to reduce their reliance on classroom and trainer-led instruction over the next two years. Why is that? Perhaps it is because they are simply not sure what else they could do instead.

When asked what methods are most likely to work, most L&D professionals pointed towards training that is integrated into the normal course of people's jobs. Half of respondents (52 per cent) said that in-house development programmes were amongst the most effective ways of delivering training, while almost as many (46 per cent) cited coaching by line managers. Two-fifths (39 per cent) pointed towards on-the-job training.

The report also revealed a third of public sector organizations anticipate greater use of e-learning across their organizations over the next two years, compared with a fifth of other organizations.

In two-fifths of organizations, talent management activities cover all or most employees, but most focus on high-potential employees and senior managers.

Half of organizations report that their economic circumstances have declined in the past 12 months, rising to three-quarters in the public sector. And the median annual training budget per employee was £276 for 2012, less than the previous year's figure of £350. The median number of formal training hours employees receive per year was 24, again a reduction on the previous year.

From the figures and anecdotal evidence, it looks as though formal training is reducing, not so much because of doubts about its efficacy, but because of budget constraints. In a way this is good news, because it is forcing L&D people to look at alternatives. It is no longer 'business as usual'.

John McGurk, learning and talent development adviser at CIPD, said: "Many of the learning approaches used by organizations are legacies of a learning environment where the classroom, courses and 'sheep-dip' learning were the order of the day. However in today's environment, the skills of continuous collaborative and connective learning are paramount. Even compliance learning and advanced skills learning needs to be re-thought with the advent of gaming and simulation.

"We need to take into account how generations learn and share knowledge and we need to understand anew the process of learning and knowledge. We need to lift our awareness of the emerging science on learning and in some cases we need to slaughter some of the sacred cows which have informed practice. Quick evaluation will become even more critical in this environment as will a fusion of coaching, leadership and change management. L&TD professionals need to lead the debate, and need to take a different perspective, calling on their own resourcefulness and creativity to push learning in new directions."

Vincent Belliveau, general manager EMEA, Cornerstone OnDemand, added: "When it comes to investing in L&D, it's critical that organizations understand their people and the learning approaches that suit them best to meet their needs. By doing so, they'll get the best return on investment as employees will be more engaged in the learning and transfer the skills into their day-to-day activities, which will ultimately support the business and its bottom line.

"It's vital that organizations don't take a 'training for training's sake' attitude but instead adopt approaches that are known to be effective ways of delivering training. It's also important that this investment can be measured, so that they can align training with business objectives. The effects of a well thought-out learning strategy can be widely felt throughout an organization, with employee engagement, job satisfaction and retention benefiting."

The problem is that training departments have not kept up with the changing times. They deliver training, while workers search and ask for the information they need, when they need it. Ultimately the conflict between these two approaches will be won by the workers.

Poor communication between L&D and the C-suite

In the past, L&D departments have tended to focus solely on delivering training. Unfortunately, instead of measuring the impact and effectiveness of the training delivered, they have measured the quality of the learning experience, how much revenue was spent on training each employee, and how many courses were completed and passed.

Those metrics hold little meaning or interest for senior executives, who measure success, not in terms of quality experiences for staff, but in performance – revenue, cash flow, profits, productivity, and the speed at which the company can deliver its services or products to market.

L&D departments have often been unwilling or unable to 'speak the language' of senior executives or to understand their needs or concerns. Consequently, those same L&D departments have been marginalized and left out of key decision-making processes. One of the most important decisions made at C-suite level is where budget is allocated within the organization to keep the organization running, so it can serve its customers. There is a huge opportunity in most organizations for L&D to become an integral part of those discussions by saying "if you want to follow this strategy, then you need capable people who can make it happen. This will involve this much L&D budget, or you won't be able to deliver on your strategy." Of course, taking this approach relies on L&D being able to make promises on employee performance, and then keep them.

One issue this raises is that the contribution of the learning and training interventions to the companies' goals has seldom been assessed, making it even more difficult for L&D departments to justify the continuing expense of training. In recent years, this situation has come under closer scrutiny.

The economic downturn has seen countless job losses and cutbacks in workforce development initiatives as companies have looked for ways to dramatically cut costs. All too often, L&D has been first in line to receive the full impact of recessionary cutbacks. After all, senior executives don't generally see L&D as something that contributes to the bottom line. Training can be 'turned off' very quickly and with minimal short-term damage. It is an easy win for someone juggling a stretched organizational budget.

At the same time, competition has become increasingly fierce. Companies are being forced to cope with situations for which they are unprepared. They desperately need employees who can and want to learn new, better ways of doing things and can master these skills quickly.

There's clearly a need for organizations to foster learning and to do everything they can to boost employee engagement. The C-suite knows this, but in many cases has lost faith in the ability of the L&D department to deliver.

The opportunity for L&D

All this has created a major opportunity for anyone involved in L&D, but it's one that involves a fundamental and radical shift in their perception of themselves and their role within the organization. Essentially, it will require L&D professionals to focus less on delivering training and more on facilitating performance capability and supporting learning.

L&D personnel need to step up and take responsibility for the capability of their organization's workforce. They need to move away from being the passive producers of training programmes and learning initiatives, and instead become proactive strategic planning partners, who understand every aspect of the organization's business.

To achieve this, L&D people need to know their organizations' strategic direction and work towards it, identifying the skills, knowledge and behaviours that people and leaders will need for the future.

They need to communicate the value of learning throughout the organization on a daily basis. Most importantly, they need to demonstrate to the C-suite exactly how the performance of the business is improved as a result of investing in both informal and formal learning initiatives. To do that, they need to understand the core competencies of their organization (those elements that give the company its competitive edge) along with its financial objectives.

When L&D aligns its strategy and tactics with the business strategy, it shows that it is a part of the business and not merely a function of it. As L&D gains more credibility within the business, it will be approached more often as a resource.

L&D people need to look beyond the number of courses they've developed or delivered, how many employees completed which course, and the costs of developing material. Instead, they should focus on delivering capability through learning, particularly informal learning. To achieve this, they need to work with all their organization's stakeholders.

Informal learning – the way that employees most like to learn and the means by which they learn the most – needs to be embraced and enhanced. L&D

needs to manage the system and environment that supports the learning that takes place throughout the organization.

Across the globe, organizations face huge challenges in the midst of the economic recession. The secret to their survival and future success lies in their employees. Right now, there is a tremendous opportunity to bring learning and development to the forefront of organizations, helping to ensure people and leaders have the capabilities they need to reach their full potential.

Chapter 2

The agile learning organization

"Learning leads to adaptations in the behaviour of employees that, if properly aligned with group and corporate goals, will allow the organization to deliver greater value to stakeholders."

Jake Reynolds

The new drivers of business success are knowledge and expertise. Whereas, in the Industrial Age, a company's main source of competitive advantage was its investments in fixed assets, such as equipment and buildings, now (and we are, according to different experts, in the Knowledge Age, Network Age, or Innovation Age), a company's main source of competitive advantage lies in its intangible assets, such as its knowledge of production, service, delivery methods and markets, its relationships with customers and suppliers, its brand value and reputation and, of course, its workforce capabilities.

Nearly all of those intangible assets are driven, one way or another, by human talent. In their book, *The Talent Powered Organization: Strategies for Globalisation, Talent Management and High Performance*, Peter Cheese and his co-authors make the point that a company's competitive advantage comes from its employees' knowledge.[17]

"In this new economic world, it is less valuable to own a piece of land than to know when to sell it and relocate activity somewhere else," Cheese said. "It is less valuable to own a factory than to know how to produce something in the most efficient way possible, less valuable to own a piece of technology than to know how to use it – or to think of a better means of production which may make that technology valueless. All of these forms of essential competitive knowledge – and many more – derive from human beings."

Research from Deloitte indicates that learning and development involves three of the top five most pressing talent concerns today (developing leaders and succession planning, managing and delivering training programmes, and creating career plans and challenging job opportunities for employees).[18]

A company's short- and long-term survival depends upon the capability of its employees – on their existing knowledge, skills and performance and, more importantly, on their ability to keep learning and thus keep expanding their capability to cope with change.

That's because what was considered an advance yesterday will be outdated by next year. Business developments happen now at the speed of light. Courses, textbooks and manuals can't keep up – they're virtually outdated by the time they're published. Formal training lags behind change. A 2011 Pew Research study found that only 55 per cent of graduates from four-year colleges believed that their education was "very useful in helping prepare them for a job or career". These findings correspond with ASTD research conducted in 2009, in which 51 per cent of those surveyed said that the skills of the current workforce do not match changes in their company's strategy, goals, markets or business models.[19]

"In more stable times, we could sit back and relax once we had learned something, secure that we could generate value from that knowledge for an indefinite period. Not anymore," say John Hagel III and his co-authors in *The Power of Pull – How Small Moves Smartly Made Can Set Big Things in Motion*.[20]

"To succeed now, we have to continually refresh our stocks of knowledge by participating in relevant 'flows' of knowledge – interactions that create knowledge or transfer it across individuals." These flows happen in any socially-fluid environment that allows organizations and individuals to get better faster by working with others, the authors say.

To illustrate the difference between stocks of knowledge and knowledge flows, they give the example of a car mechanic trying to keep up with the rapidly-changing technologies embedded in the cars of today. With only the training received at the outset of his or her career the mechanic would be "hopelessly lost" with today's computer systems. Even taking additional training programmes or reading manuals would be unlikely to enable the mechanic to fully keep up to date.

"There would likely be a need to connect with other mechanics and perhaps even the manufacturer to problem-solve unanticipated issues with the cars coming in for repairs," they say. Without access to these flows of knowledge, the mechanics would soon be unable to do their job.

Consequently, employees today are becoming more active in professional groups, where they can pick up knowledge that will prove useful in their work through discussions with others. Their knowledge evolves and they also learn to ask questions of the groups in a way that gets better responses.

The only real way for companies to increase their competitiveness is if their employees learn in real time and from one another.

Sam Herring, CEO of Intrepid Learning, says, "We need to better prepare, train, and inspire successful self-directed learners to meet today's challenges. As I see it, there are two big questions to consider. First, what are the critical 21st century skills that the workforce of tomorrow needs to develop and master today? Secondly, how can we improve our learning methods to enable the self-directed learner to thrive in this new environment?"[21]

"As leaders responsible for designing and implementing successful business strategies, and preparing our workforces to shape and execute them, we face clear challenges", says Herring. "We must find new ways to help yesterday's knowledge workers take responsibility for their own development, and to see that development as central to not just their employer's value creation, but their own value creation as well."

Although employees' ability to conduct 'knowledge work' has been greatly enhanced by advances in technology such as cloud-computing, advanced mobile applications and devices, and rapidly expanding social networks, they need more than just the tools.

Organizations need to help the knowledge workers of yesterday move beyond their comfort zones to become the innovation workers of tomorrow. It is critical that they embrace self-directed, continuous development to differentiate their skills and make themselves invaluable contributors to the economy. This, in turn, will help their organizations accelerate business results, spark innovation, improve performance, and drive growth.

While, previously, knowledge workers have been required to master their specific area of expertise, their expertise in one subject is no longer sufficient. Nowadays, they need to be more agile, curious, and committed to continuous learning, because their employers need to be able to identify new opportunities, design creative solutions and bring them to market. Companies now need innovative workers, rather than mere knowledge workers.

As far as employees are concerned, they need to take responsibility for continually developing their skills and knowledge to demonstrate their value to organizations and maintain their employability. The emphasis now is on self-empowered learning rather than learning that is pushed by an organization. Employees have to continuously prove their worth.

The arrival of the agile learning organization

There is an oft-used quote from Charles Darwin; "It is not the strongest of the species that survives nor the most intelligent, but the one most responsive to change." Another pithy and relevant quote is from W. Edwards Deming; "It is not necessary to change. Survival is not mandatory."

Organizations need to reinvent the way they learn. To sustain competitiveness, they need to be able to learn at or above the speed of change, and we all know that the change around us is accelerating. Even just to keep pace with their competitors, they must accelerate the speed at which they collect, share and implement knowledge.

There is a strong correlation between organizations with a learning culture (the collective practices that encourage the sharing of information and all forms of people development) and measurable business outcomes.

A leading US-based human resource research and consulting firm, Bersin & Associates, has revealed that organizations with a strong learning culture have 37 per cent greater employee productivity, are 32 per cent more likely to be first to market, and are 17 per cent more likely to be market leaders in their segment.[22]

The same research shows that most companies do not understand this area well, despite the opportunity to drive tremendous performance improvements with almost no additional expense.

A 2008 study by the American Society of Training and Development (ASTD) reported that informal learning's existence is positively correlated to performance.[23] In fact, 46 per cent of respondents to the ASTD study stated that informal learning enhanced performance to a high or very high extent. The study also found a significant correlation between the degree to which informal learning occurs in organizations and their reported market performance.

The study executive summary states: "Overall, these and other findings suggest that although informal learning remains a poorly understood and measured process, it is becoming increasingly important and has considerable untapped potential. If organizations can harness the potential of informal learning, it can become an unusually powerful and cost-effective performance tool in coming years."

Organizational learning agility is an enterprise capability that requires deliberate and systematic design, including such essential elements as culture, structure, process and technology support.

Learning can no longer be limited to classroom training or even e-learning and other delivery methods. Integration, speed, reach and real-time connectivity must be built into the learning environment. The way that organizations think about learning must change towards an agile learning environment. In effect, this means that training, performance support, distributed learning, communities of practice, knowledge banks and indeed any contributors to learning must be integrated and playing a blended and synergistic harmony.

Essentials of an agile learning strategy

The primary goal of an agile learning environment is to enhance on-the-job capability in a way that improves performance and thus results. Several fundamental concepts and best practices are key to creating this new learning environment. Its critical components include alignment, full-service learning, integration, learning at the point of need and learning partnerships.

The most important first step for an L&D professional is to ensure that all learning initiatives and activities align with the business goals of the organization. This is the only reliable route to senior leadership support.

Everything related to learning – courses, learning modules, consulting practices, workshops – must clearly contribute to the organization's success. There must be a clear line of sight between the intended outcomes of the learning intervention and the vision and mission of the organization.

Until recently, most training programmes took place in the classroom; they were delivered away from the job and were one-dimensional, with a set time, place and location. Training in groups was the common format. There were few one-on-one mentoring, coaching, follow-up or other individual-focused methods. Career-long learning and development was primarily an individual's responsibility. After a formal classroom training intervention, it was left to the individual employee to continue learning or not.

What used to be limited to training should now be thought of as a multi-disciplined approach or architecture, whose purpose is to provide learning at the point of need. All learning and development activities must be thoughtfully and deliberately integrated by an L&D person's overarching learning strategy.

Such a strategy will also provide employees with more control over their learning opportunities – encompassing, complementing, and supplementing formal training with continuous learning activities, performance support and knowledge-sharing activities.

Using a multi-dimensional approach, courses should be integrated into the learning environment so they are not separate events. Focusing on performance and the total needs of the workforce, learning should be used to provide core skill sets and competencies, meta-knowledge (how to learn) and the ability to access knowledge around the clock. The end goal is employee capability.

Performance support provides an additional learning asset to the workforce. To provide this expert consulting service, a high degree of job knowledge and expertise is required from L&D professionals, who should be able to deliver mentoring and coaching and share critical best practices on the job and at the point of need. Distributed learning, powered with web-based technology and learning management systems, including e-learning courses, modules and other technology-based learning activities, now has a worldwide reach. Finally, the knowledge-sharing framework adds the critical ingredients of connectivity, on-demand learning and reach-back capability to complete the agile learning environment.

Knowledge-sharing

A knowledge-sharing system provides connectivity and agility to the learning environment. It does this by:

- Saving time by providing direct access to policies, procedures, lessons learned, changing practices and the collective knowledge of the organization
- Pointing out best practices and lessons within the organization, which boosts productivity
- Finding and using proven practices and sharing lessons learned across the workforce, which improves effectiveness
- Giving access to relevant, current, authoritative and valid information sources, which accelerates problem-solving
- Connecting and sharing resources within the organization to include its suppliers, which leverages expertise and experience
- Providing access to resources and opportunities that help employees grow professionally, which enhances professional development.

To achieve performance improvement, all courses, lessons, continuous learning modules and knowledge-sharing assets should be functionally and collectively designed and integrated, so the whole is greater than the sum of the parts.

A new agile learning environment must include real-time access to subject-matter experts, knowledge at the point of need and on-the-job access to all relevant tools. As part of a knowledge-sharing system, learning and development organizations can focus on the learning-on-demand needs of the workforce by making smart business templates and new tools, such as search technologies, instantly available to field organizations and their respective communities.

NASA is a perfect example of an organization that has, by necessity, become an agile learning organization. In 2000, the US Congress, which funds NASA, had called on the agency to develop appropriate knowledge-management tools to reduce the risk of future mission failures and to address the impending retirement issue.

NASA faced a major problem – many of its most experienced scientists and engineers were nearing retirement. Jeanne Holm, its Chief Knowledge Architect, said it was apparent that the institution would suffer if it didn't have systems in place to retain more of what those employees knew.[24]

"Many of these people are the most experienced project managers – the people who worked on Apollo [the mission to the moon] and built the first space shuttle. Yet, we have few programmes designed to bring their wisdom into our institutional memory," she said.

Back then, some of her own team members didn't seem to understand the significance of the knowledge-loss issue. Until 2002, most of NASA's knowledge-management tools were IT systems, but the IT systems alone could not address NASA's mandate. Instead, the agency had to change its culture.

"The problem is IT systems don't address the critical need for the most experienced people to mentor and train others or to share tacit knowledge from one mission to another."

Without that critical knowledge, missions would fail or be delayed or cancelled.

"For example, assessing risk in designing spacecraft components is one of the most difficult tasks; novices can learn this only from experienced engineers and scientists, or trial and error."

What the agency needed was a cultural shift in the way experiential knowledge was cultivated and managed.

Such a shift was going to be a hard pitch, since at the time the agency was $4 billion over budget on the International Space Station.

Another problem was trying to convince engineers and scientists within the various centres to share knowledge.

"Competition among centers for projects and funding can be an engine for creativity but it also sustains a culture of privatizing knowledge. Scientists and engineers sometimes don't include material in their reports that might compromise their competitive advantage."

One HR initiative was to recognize and reward knowledge sharing and mentoring, but it didn't have widespread political support within the agency.

Holm and her team faced major challenges.

- How could they transfer information from one mission to another between generations of people who entered and left the agency: some missions take 50 years to complete? Long-duration projects tended to have older technologies that required extensive knowledge of their original construction. NASA needed a way to capture, organize and store knowledge so that it was accessible to the right people at the right time.
- How could they get hugely diverse, geographically distributed communities to work together on complex space missions? This posed a politically tricky problem, since other government agencies were involved, making it important to understand how and when to share technical information with international and industrial partners who were also often its competitors.
- How should they manage their existing knowledge? At that time, NASA had four million public web pages and was averaging two billion hits per month from such diverse visitors as schoolchildren and potential business partners interested in participating in future space missions.

The strategy that was developed was based on a performance-orientated definition of knowledge management – one that would get the right information to the right people at the right time and help them create knowledge and share and act upon information in ways that would measurably improve NASA and its partners' performance.

Part of that strategy would be accomplished through clever IT solutions and improved access to NASA's explicit information, while the larger part would involve capturing the tacit knowledge of its workforce and effecting a cultural change that would encourage people to share what they knew.

To achieve that, they first set about improving the existing documentation – the Lessons Learned Information System (LLIS).

An earlier review of the LLIS system had recognized that managers were reluctant to share negative lessons, fearing they might not be viewed as good project managers. Also, there was little time for lessons learning to take place.

A survey revealed that managers didn't routinely identify, collect or share lessons learnt. Instead, managers identified programme reviews and informal discussions with colleagues as their principal source for lessons learning.

One centre official said the lessons covered so many topics that it was difficult to search for an applicable lesson. Similarly, another said it was difficult to find the relevant lessons amongst so much information.

Holm and her team developed web-based internal-use portals that employees could use to search efficiently for the information they needed on an ongoing basis. Those pages could be tailored to access project-related information from all over the agency, universities and industry. Several web-based tools were developed to make it much easier for project team members from different centres to collaborate.

Through a Knowledge Sharing Initiative (KSI), NASA's Academy of Program and Project Leadership (APPL) supported best-practice communities and a culture of knowledge sharing through grass-roots efforts across the agency. KSI worked with centres to identify the best managers and bring them together to share project-related stories in a series of workshops held twice a year.

In 2003, NASA turned its diverse 3,000 websites, comprising more than two million web pages, thousands of databases, and millions of online reports, into a single public portal.[25]

NASA's administrator, Sean O'Keefe, said he wanted to provide a single face of the institute to the public, and that required a single entry point. This would then branch into a variety of diverse audiences, targeting media, schoolchildren, educators and the public. He gave the Knowledge Management team four weeks to get it done.

It was launched on January 31, 2003, a few hours before Space Shuttle Columbia was destroyed upon re-entry to earth. Within the first 48 hours, the portal had received 225 million hits.

NASA's portal strategy is just one aspect of the agency's attempts at knowledge management. NASA's bottom-line product is knowledge, according to Holm. Its intellectual capital provides its source of competitive advantage.

"The stuff that NASA creates is what writes science textbooks for kids and colleges", Holm relates. "We have the highest-educated work force in the US government. It's really important that we capture those things as they occur and capture them over time. So when others want to look at historical timelines, they can get a sense of what was going on at a certain point in science history."

The agency's 50-person knowledge management team supports 120 communities of practice, enables remote collaboration, provides collaborative tools for virtual teams and encourages storytelling. NASA also is beginning to examine how to reward and recognize knowledge sharing and is creating a Lessons Learned Knowledge Network.

As Holm states, "At NASA, the knowledge that helps us do our work is everywhere. We take a very distributed approach to knowledge management by helping people get done what they need to in their part of the organization."

Learning partnerships

Learning is a continuum (from formal to informal) that includes many important aspects in addition to training; such as knowledge sharing, performance support and career-long learning. These cannot just be left to individual employee initiatives – they must be a shared responsibility within the agile learning organization. They must be planned, resourced, managed and thoughtfully deployed. This requires a mindset in which learning now becomes the responsibility, not just of L&D, but also of supervisors, line managers, employees, stakeholders, and senior leaders. They must all become partners in learning.

L&D has to expand its scope of responsibility beyond training (classroom, online or hybrid), into performance support, knowledge sharing of best practices and acting as an expert consultant to the rest of the organization about all things relating to learning. It must distribute learning to reach larger populations through emerging technologies, providing the continuity and connectivity that are essential in an agile learning environment.

This multidimensional approach provides the right amount of content, at the right time, at the right place and in the right format. The integration of learning at the point of work with real-time access to expertise and knowledge is setting in motion a huge shift from the traditional classroom environment of the 20th century to the total learning environment of the 21st century.

Factors that limit or enhance learning agility

Studies by TRClark, a research, consulting and training company, show there are five primary factors, described below, that interact to promote or hinder organizational learning agility.[26]

Intelligence function

This is the organization's capacity to survey and interpret its entire business ecosystem (including both internal and external competitive environments). The intelligence function interprets information for the strategy function, which feeds the learning function.

To become agile, organizations need to establish a comprehensive and systematic process for gathering, integrating and interpreting intelligence from a variety of sources. Critically, there must be direct communication between the intelligence function, the strategy function, and the learning function. If not, the learning function won't have enough time to respond to the needs of the organization and will remain a passive, tactical part of the business.

Learning mindset

This comprises the prevailing assumptions, beliefs and dispositions relating to the way people learn.

Organizations and individuals are being forced towards a dynamic learning mind-set. Dynamic learning is rapid, adaptive, collaborative and self-directed learning at the moment of need. This mind-set recognizes learning as the source of competitive advantage.

The danger with dynamic learning is that, without support or guidance, the search for knowledge may be inefficient or ineffective. Employees may need help to avoid over-saturation, non-productive or irrelevant learning.

It may be necessary to provide 'how to learn' solutions, particularly in regard to using all the tools available via the internet.

Leadership behaviour

This means the dominant patterns of leadership within the organization. Leaders need to be comfortable portraying themselves as competent simply by virtue of their ability to learn and adapt, rather than on the basis of their current knowledge and skills. In other words, they need to model patterns of high-performance learning as they move through learning and change cycles. They must be aware that their ability to protect the value of the organization is based on its willingness to learn and adapt, and the biggest risk an organization can take is to cease to learn.

Organizational support

There are five 'moments of need' when learners need support:

1. Learning how to do something for the first time.
2. Learning more, based on prior experience.
3. Learning at the moment when learners apply what they have learned in the context of workflow.
4. Learning when things change in order to adapt to new ways of doing things.
5. Learning when things go wrong in order to solve a problem.

An organization should have support mechanisms in place for all five of these situations. Collaborative learning is a key part of an agile learning organization. So too is the sharing and application of collective knowledge and skills within the organization and beyond. Collective knowledge and skills covers information that employees have, as well as what has been captured and stored. It should be made useful in a form that is accessible and adaptive to individual needs.

Learning technology

There is so much new technology coming along that organizations must guard against being techno-dazzled, and make sure they seek out technology that supports the above four factors in attaining specific outcomes in a practical and usable way.

Learning leaders

It is clear from the above studies that the leadership of any organization has a profound impact on its ability to be agile, to learn faster than the speed of change, and hence to survive. Organizational development expert Edgar H. Stein maintains that unless leaders become learners themselves, transformational learning will not occur.[27]

"The evidence is mounting that real change does not begin until the organization experiences some real threat of pain that in some way dashes its expectations or hopes. This threat can come from a number of places internally, including from the CEO, or it can come from competitors. Whatever its source, this threat of pain creates high levels of learning anxiety and survival anxiety, ultimately prompting the organization to launch a serious change programme.

"Not surprisingly, it is often the CEO and other executives who feel most threatened by any new learning because it reveals their behaviour to be dysfunctional.

"Unless leaders become learners themselves – unless they can acknowledge their own vulnerabilities and uncertainties – then transformational learning will never take place.

"When leaders become genuine learners, they set a good example and help to create a psychologically safe environment for others."

There is, however, much more going on than leaders setting a good learning example.

Leadership and learning – and their interdependence

Leadership is often seen as an answer to all sorts of problems. How often have you heard something like "We are in a crisis because of [insert your favourite problem, such as economy, slow markets, reduced budgets, poor products, competition, low morale and so on], and we need leadership. It is the only way out of this mess."

The cry goes up for leadership, and for leaders who will swoop in with capes flying and save the day.

And yet leadership does not stand on its own as a panacea. Organizations are complex systems and there are dependencies that come into play. There is a strong link between leadership and learning, and the interesting thing is that it is a two-way link.

Leadership <> Learning

It is quite possible L&D have not yet made this connection, and so may be throwing money and resources into leadership development, only to be left wondering why the results are not quite as good as they wanted, or indeed as good as they promised to the board.

This connection is not so obvious until you add the middle link in the chain

Leadership <> Engagement <> Learning

So let's look at these links as we travel along the chain, there and back.

Leadership > Engagement

This one takes little explaining and is almost a bedrock of faith in the way leadership is promoted and evangelized. And it's true. Indeed, you could say that the sole purpose of leadership is to get people engaged: to engender within them a desire to participate in the leader's vision, and go the extra mile.

It is this desire to participate that is the key. The leader proposes a vision, a task, a project in such a way that people want to contribute; they want to get involved, and to see it come to fruition and succeed. They want to be part of something significant, something they would most likely not wholeheartedly support were it not for the leader.

Of course, if there is no leadership, there will be little engagement (except perhaps that engendered by a basic worker compliance that is sufficient to ensure they receive a pay slip at the end of each month).

Engagement > Learning

Let's assume we have engagement. We have people who want to participate and contribute. What is their next step?

They will do what they need to do to get involved. They will find out what they need to find out. They will speak to whoever they need to speak to. They will put in the time, and they will put in the effort. And they will learn what they need to learn so their contribution can be effective and meaningful.

Given that a leader's vision is different from the status quo, or it wouldn't really be a vision, let alone a motivating one, it will involve change, which will usually involve new skills and new ways of doing things. Change requires learning, so participating in a leader's vision will almost always involve learning.

But if the engagement is not there, why would anyone bother to learn?

Learning in adults tends to be a goal-orientated process, especially in the workplace. We do things for a reason. When we have a goal that we wish to achieve, we learn what we need to learn in order to achieve that goal.

If there is no goal, no desire to participate, no engagement... then learning dies. And if training is delivered that does not relate to a present goal, the learning is not received. You can't teach someone something they don't want to know, no matter how much you might dress it up with phrases like "You will need this later".

Learning > Engagement

Now let's look at this connection from the other direction – the effect of learning on engagement.

When people learn new things in their pursuit of a goal, and it makes the pursuit of that goal easier, the goal seems closer and more attainable. A goal that you can reach out and almost touch is more motivating than one that seems impossible because you just can't imagine ever being able to do it. The more you learn and the more capable you become of contributing meaningfully to a leader's goal, the more engaged with that goal you will become. It is exciting being part of something bigger than you, and being able to contribute to it. Learning and capability potentiate engagement.

But what if you can't learn what you need to learn and know in order to participate? What if the barriers to learning are too high? What if the information you need is not available? What then?

And what if you can learn, but find the barriers to implementing the learning are high? For example, mistakes are not tolerated, so trying new things is dangerous, or systems are set up in such a way as to stifle any change. What then?

You feel frustrated. The desire to go for the goal dissipates, and the engagement wilts like a plant without water. The desire to participate fades away, and in many cases is replaced by cynicism as a response to any further attempts at engagement. The employee feels unsupported by the organization and by their manager, and they start looking for the door.

Lack of opportunity, either to learn or to apply learning, becomes a restraining force on engagement.

Engagement > Leadership

What is the effect of engagement on leadership?

When people are engaged, they will follow the vision; they will follow the leader because they like where the leader is taking them. The more they follow a leader, the more they will allow themselves to be influenced by that leader. Engagement and leadership feed off each other.

But what if the engagement hits a stumbling block? What if some other factor reduces the power of engagement? What if there are barriers to follower behaviour, such as lack of the proper equipment, lack of clarity over decision boundaries, or ineffective work processes?

People will lose their desire to participate. People won't follow that vision, that leader. If the ability to engage is restricted in some way, the leader will have no followers. A leader with no followers is simply someone walking their path alone.

Leadership <> Engagement <> Learning

Now we can see the interdependence up and down this chain. We can see how leadership can impact upon learning, not because the leader espouses learning, but simply because they are a leader with a vision and followers.

We can also see how learning can impact the effects of leadership. It can act as an accelerator or a brake on the primary output of leadership, which is engagement.

If your learning environment is not functioning well, pouring resources into developing leadership will never have the impact it could have. Organizations need to ensure that it is easier to follow the leaders, than not follow.

Engagement without enablement will get you nowhere.

The learnscape

The term learnscape was coined during the 1970s to denote areas set aside in schools where pupils could interact with the environment and learn from that interaction. It could have been a special plot in the grounds where they planted seeds, a frog pond to observe the frog's life cycle, or an ant farm in the classroom. The whole concept was about interaction and the involvement of all concerned: pupils, teachers and also parents and the community.

The term has evolved somewhat for use in an organizational context, but it still embodies the central ideas of collaboration, involvement and integration across different groups and stakeholders.

Every organization has a learning environment, or learnscape. It is the eco-system that comprises all that is within or around an organization that has an impact on learning. Employees, and sometimes customers and suppliers, exist within this learnscape; how much or how easily they learn is dependent on how well the learnscape is functioning.

The learnscape, and how well it functions, will determine if an organization's leaders can be successful. If the learnscape is not functioning well, it takes an extraordinary leader to engage people sufficiently to succeed. Conversely, if the learnscape is working well, people can follow a leader more easily, and the quality of leadership is not such an issue.

A well-functioning learnscape is like a catalyst for the reaction that transforms leadership into engagement, with all its benefits. It speeds up the process and in some cases is a requirement for making the process possible.

Now, here is the critical thing about a learnscape, and it's something that many people don't realize and need to understand: very little of the learning that happens is due to formal training. The majority of what people know how to do in order to fulfil their job roles, they have learnt outside the classroom or any formal training initiative. Most of the learning that goes on within any learnscape is informal learning, and this is especially the case with learning done in the moment by people following a leader's vision. They just find out and figure out what they need in order to participate. That's informal learning.

You can't force informal learning. All you can do is provide a backdrop and an environment in which it is more likely to occur. To do this you need to manage your learnscape.

A learnscape is a learning ecosystem. You don't create it; it is already there. You tend it and manage it to enhance it. This is analogous to a garden. You don't create a garden out of thin air: the ground already exists, but you can tend it to bring harmony and beauty. You do this by ensuring the garden provides all that the plants need to thrive, including nutrients, water, shelter and so on. Gardeners do not control the growth of a plant directly, any more than managers can control learning. Gardeners know they can influence, but not control, the plants. All the same, they'll be delighted when a plant bursts into bloom unexpectedly. It's the same with a learnscape.

If people are working in an environment where they can flourish, most of them will. There are lots of elements you can introduce into a landscape to make things grow better, but how you introduce them makes a difference. You can pour fertilizer onto a garden, but if it's not soluble in water, it won't make any difference to the plants. It's not bioavailable. It's the same with the learnscape. You can pour information into a learnscape, but if it's not available for people to use, it won't be of any benefit to them.

I see this happening in some companies. They say, "We have a glut of information. It's all on the Intranet." I ask them to show me and often they can't find it because it's not easily accessible. So, if you're feeding information into a learnscape, you need to make sure that the information is bioavailable.

With a plant, you can put a trellis up a wall for it to grow up, but you can't make it grow the way you want it to. It will grow the way it pleases. You can direct plants, but there's always a point at which the plants grow the way they want. It's the same with people. You can encourage career progression. You can encourage learning and development in a certain direction, but ultimately it's down to individuals to do what they want. Some will use the information and produce results and some, unfortunately, will not.

With new people, you can nurture their introduction into the organization, just as a gardener protects and nurtures seedlings until they are strong enough to cope. You can take newcomers through induction processes and protect them until they're strong enough to stand on their own. For example, they might go through a training course on product knowledge, or shadow a veteran before you let them loose with real life customers.

Occasionally in a garden, you may find that a plant is doing badly or that weeds have begun to flourish. What do you do? You remove the poor performing plant or weeds. In an organization, people who aren't pulling their weight are usually removed if all attempts at helping them to do better have failed. Not everybody is right for every company.

Moment of truth

What happens in your organization when an employee wants to do something they have not done before and they don't quite know how to do it?

This is a 'moment of truth', and these come often when people are following a leader on a new path of change and success.

The phrase 'moment of truth' was popularized by Jan Carlzon, CEO of Scandinavian Airline Systems and architect of its spectacular turnaround. For him, it meant that moment when one of his employees interacted with a customer making a reservation, checking in or being served a meal. The brand of the airline was at stake during every such interaction, because the customer would form or change their impression about his company. He focused on making sure that his employees were capable of handling those moments of truth well, so that after each one, he would have another happy customer.

When following a leader, the moments of truth are those moments when an employee comes to a fork in the road. Down one road are actions that support and contribute to the success of the leader's vision. Down the other are at best indifference and perhaps even cynicism and sabotage of the leader's vision.

Which is the easier road for the employee to travel?

Manage your learnscape so the employee finds it easiest to take the road that leads to engagement. Consider this quote from Jan Carlzon:

"An individual without information can't take responsibility. An individual with information can't help but take responsibility."

Invest in your learnscape

Many people talk about the need to invest in their people: "People are our greatest asset… we must invest in them, and pour knowledge and skills into them." L&D looks into the oracle of their Learning Management System (LMS) and decides who needs to learn what, based on their role in the organization.

There is nothing inherently wrong with this approach, except that it focuses attention on individuals because they appear as line items on the LMS screen. Consequently, L&D practitioners lose sight of the fact that these employees are operating within a learnscape and there is far more that is relevant to their capability to do a job than is indicated by a row of tick boxes on screen.

Think instead about investing in your learnscape to improve the whole learning environment within your organization. Your learnscape stays, even as employees come and go. So invest in what stays with the organization. Invest so that employees can reach out and learn wherever, whenever and however they need. If you have the right learning environment, it is actually easier for people to learn than not learn. It is easier for them to take that fork in the road that leads to success for the organization.

Managers in the middle

Who has the biggest influence on how well the learnscape operates and on motivation and engagement?

Answer: your team supervisors and line managers.

Studies show that an employee's direct supervisor has the greatest impact on their performance, and on their loyalty and motivation. But survey after survey delivers data showing that far more employees are disengaged than engaged, far more managers are thought to be poor than good, and managers are more likely to douse the flames of enthusiasm than fan them. Something clearly needs fixing in many, if not most, organizations.

And it is not just a leadership problem, though many would have you subscribe to that view. It is also a learning problem, because leadership and learning are interdependent. The solution lies with the team supervisors and middle managers.

Chapter 3

What is informal learning?

*"Informal and formal learning are the end points of a continuum.
On one end, formal learning is like riding a bus: The driver decides
where the bus is going, while the passengers are along for the ride.
On the opposite end, informal learning is like riding a bike: the rider
chooses the destination, the speed, and the route."*

Jay Cross

Informal learning is a rather confusing notion, because the definitions vary and the term is bandied about by many who have not really even defined what 'learning' is, let alone some variety of it called 'informal'. So let's first take a quick look at the concept of learning

In the 60s and 70s, the standard psychology textbooks defined learning in terms of a change in behaviour. Learning was approached as an outcome and was the end product of a learning process. The change in behaviour could be seen, so learning was couched in terms of change. This somewhat simplistic view had a few drawbacks and gave rise to some obvious questions:

1. Is the change in behaviour really required in order to know that learning has happened? Or could the potential to change be sufficient to signify learning, and if so, how do you know learning has happened?

2. Are there things other than learning that can cause behaviour to change, and thus we don't know for sure if learning actually took place?

You will still find today this idea that learning and change are interchangeable in some way, but there is more to it than that.

If you ask people what they think learning means, the answers will vary widely, but will tend to belong to one or the other of two concepts.

The first is that learning is about memorizing information so it can be recalled. It is about knowing a lot of things, or having access to a lot of internally-stored information. It also covers the area of skills and methods that have been internalized so they can be used at will (for example, a dance routine).

Thought of in these terms, learning is a bit like shopping: you can go out and get learning and it becomes your possession.

The second concept, which is often offered up after a little more thought, is that learning is about making sense of information, or abstracting meaning from evidence. It involves making relationships between bits of information and the real world. It is about 'joining the dots' to get a new understanding or interpretation of reality.

This is a much more personal view of learning, as it is about something that happens internally within the learner. It is something people do to make sense of the world around them. It is something that adds value and depth and scope to the 'shopping' concept of learning, and takes the learning further.

One question that arises about learning is how much people are conscious of what they are doing when they are learning. And does it matter if they are aware that they are learning? If they are unaware, is it still learning? This question begins to lead us into the informal areas of learning.

Alan Rogers sets out two contrasting approaches: task conscious or acquisition learning and learning-conscious or formalized learning.[28] The first is the kind of learning that happens when you are conscious of the task, though you may be unconscious of any explicit learning taking place. Rogers says it is "concrete, immediate and confined to a specific activity; it is not concerned with general principles". It is going on all the time and it is how we learn to be a parent or run a home. It is the 'side-effect of life' learning mentioned at the very start of the book. It is the accumulation of experience.

Learning-conscious or formalized learning arises when there is full awareness of learning as an outcome, so it is 'educative' learning. The task may not be a learning task, but learning is one of the desired outputs of the task and the task is set up so that learning can take place.

It is clear that both types of learning can take place at the same time and within the same context. They can also be seen as forming the ends of a continuum. Rogers defines the continuum in this way:

"At one extreme lie those unintentional and usually accidental learning events which occur continuously as we walk through life. Next comes incidental learning – unconscious learning through acquisition methods which occurs in the course of some other activity... Then there are various activities in which we are somewhat more conscious of learning, experiential activities arising from immediate life-related concerns, though even here the focus is still on the task... Then come more purposeful activities – occasions where we set out to learn something in a more systematic way, using whatever comes to hand for that purpose, but often deliberately disregarding engagement with teachers and formal institutions of learning... Further along the continuum lie the self-directed learning projects on which there is so much literature... More formalized and generalized (and consequently less contextualized) forms of learning are the distance and open education programmes, where some elements of acquisition learning are often built into the designed learning programme. Towards the further extreme lie more formalized learning programmes of highly decontextualized learning, using material common to all the learners without paying any regard to their individual preferences, agendas or needs. There are of course no clear boundaries between any of these categories."

As you look through the continuum described by Rogers, you can see that at one end is what most people in L&D are referring to with the term 'informal learning', and at the other end is 'formal learning'. His description also makes it obvious that there is no clear cut boundary between the two.

We need to approach learning holistically and, although it is useful for operational purposes to separate informal and formal learning, it must always be remembered that they co-exist on this continuum.

So what is informal learning?

Considerable time and effort is invested in formal training programmes by many organizations. Many still don't realize that employees only learn about 10 to 30 per cent of what they know from training programmes. The majority of employees' learning happens informally back in the office or on the shop floor.

Informal learning is any learning or collaboration that takes place outside of a class, seminar or workshop, beyond the scope of a self-study course, and away from any environment recognized as part of formal learning.

It happens as a result of interactions between people. Quite often, it is not even recognized as 'learning', because a lot of it is an exchange of tacit knowledge – "the sharing of knowledge gained through experience with another who hasn't yet had those experiences".[29]

Informal learning is something that many people are talking about, but it seems that very few grasp how important it is in the work context.

It's been said the water cooler is the new corporate university, and what may seem like idle chatter should often be encouraged, not stamped out.

When you look back at your most powerful and deep learning, it's informal. It's in context. It has meaning.

Reflect for a moment on how you have learnt most of your professional skills. I suspect it will be a mix of watching master performers, trial and error, sessions with friends, faking it, reading magazines, calling the helpdesk, asking the person in the next cubicle, listening to stories, composing a story, burning your finger on a hot stove, waking up with an inspiration, visiting a museum, pursuing a hobby, noticing and reflecting and just talking to people.

This is natural learning: learning from others when you feel the need to do so.

Informal learning in the workplace is neither the training department's job nor a human resource function: nurturing informal learning is an implicit part of every manager's job. L&D's job is to make it happen easily and seamlessly within the work context.

What's more, informal learning is the way people like to learn (even though most probably won't be consciously aware they are learning). In general, workers do not like training. They do, however, often say they do, because they get to go away to a nice hotel and escape their desk for a day or two.

Push versus pull learning

Training is 'push learning', which happens when an outside source or authority chooses the curriculum for a learner. It comes with the implied belief, "You need to learn this". Obviously, there are situations where push learning is necessary, such as learning safety routines, for example. In a teacher- or trainer-centric learning system, push learning reigns. However, this kind of learning goes against the natural way people learn. The human brain is designed to learn on an opt-in basis – the individual controls the motive and reason for learning. When that individual is interested in a subject or situation, he or she learns faster, retains the information for longer and is more likely to integrate the knowledge into his or her knowledge base.

Push models treat people as passive consumers whose needs can be anticipated and shaped by centralized decision-makers, say organizational learning experts John Hagel and John Seeley Brown.[30] Pull models, however, treat people as networked creators who are uniquely positioned to transform uncertainty from a problem into an opportunity. Pull models are ultimately designed to accelerate capability building by participants, helping them to learn as well as innovate, by pursuing trajectories of learning that are tailored to their specific needs.

Hagel says the dominant model for institutions today is one that pushes, rather than pulls. "Virtually everyone operates on the model that says that your first challenge is to forecast or predict demand and then to organize to make sure all the right people and right resources are in the right place to meet demand," he says.

The model requires a tightly integrated and executed system, which is increasingly difficult to maintain in a rapidly-changing environment. "For a variety of reasons having to do with long-term trends playing out in the world, the ability to predict and forecast is more and more challenged and there's a need... to think about pull platforms, which allow you to draw out the right people and right resources wherever they're needed, whenever they're needed," he suggests.

In a pull platform, talent development emphasizes on-the-job learning and informal structures, rather than a formal training programme. Pull learning gives people the ability to confront challenges and draw out the resources needed to develop solutions.

"The learning is actually a by-product of facing unexpected challenges and ever-increasing performance requirements," Hagel claims. "If you really took that seriously, you would end up rethinking all aspects of the company from operations, how you design the organization, even what kind of business strategy you would pursue, and certainly what kind of technology platforms you would use to support them in their work environments."

Nick Milton blogged about eight demand-side knowledge management principles, based on his and his colleagues' experiences as knowledge management consultants.[31] These principles are about the learner:

1. People don't pay attention to knowledge until they actually need it.
2. People value knowledge that they request more highly than knowledge that is unsolicited.
3. People won't use knowledge, unless they trust its provenance.
4. Knowledge has to be reviewed in the user's own context before it can be received.
5. One of the biggest barriers to accepting new knowledge is old knowledge.
6. Knowledge has to be adapted before it can be adopted.
7. Knowledge will be more effective the more personal it is.
8. They won't really know it until they do it.

If you think about push learning or formal training with these principles in mind, there is a massive disconnect. For example, how often are training courses delivered to learners at the moment they need that specific information? Pull style learning is far more suited to satisfying these principles and this helps explain a lot of learner frustration and the growing use of learner 'workarounds'.

According to extensive clandestine research by the co-authors of *Hacking Work: Breaking Stupid Rules for Smart Results*, Bill Jensen and Josh Klein, between one-third and two-thirds of employees are meeting their learning needs by working around L&D and IT departments.

Stymied by their organization's infrastructure – the tools and processes employees are supposed to use to get their work done – they do what they can to find ways to get the work done. While these tools and processes are designed to help the company succeed, they are not built for the success of the individuals who do the work, say Jensen and Klein. They comment that "Business's failure to deal with this obvious problem is one of its biggest problems."

In an article in *Chief Learning Officer Magazine*[32] the pair said "Learning and development is rarely learner-centred, for example. Once we get past the executives who get five-star concierge-like support, study after study finds that most in the workforce are not getting the tailored learning and development they so desperately need to excel.

"What do your learners find outside of your company? They find that IT and training play together quite well. For example, Apple's store has over 300,000 apps, thousands of which deliver on-the-fly tutorials plus developmental and assessment tools tailored to every need, many of which are free.

"Through coaching portals, the expertise of world-class coaches and how-to gurus like Ram Charam, Marshall Goldsmith and David Allen is available for peanuts. With social networking, most everyone can reach out to peers for advice on most any how-to, and Google is now every employee's adjunct professor."

Faced with workplace obstacles, employees create their own workarounds or hacks to get the information they need, say Jensen and Klein. Gary and Sean are two people they interviewed.

"Gary found that what L&D provided was so lacking that he built his own internal wiki and started sharing it. His wiki went viral within the company and produced critical bottom-line results, so senior management had no choice but to sanction it after the fact.

"Sean created computer training for his company's project management and knowledge-sharing tools. He knew that what the CIO [Chief Information Officer] had commissioned from outside vendors was a waste of everyone's time. So he asked for permission to test a prototype that his team was working on. Within a year, Sean's prototype had gone viral throughout the company and absolutely no one was using the CIO-approved pet project."

After several years of secret meetings with thousands of people given the promise of anonymity, Jensen and Klein found that these kinds of unofficial hacks and projects are extremely common and happening everywhere.

"And as long as HR and IT are not worker-centred, these kinds of workarounds are only going to increase," they predicted. "Learners are only working around organizational barriers because it's the only way they can get the personalized training and development they need.

"Up to two-thirds of the workforce knows what's blind to you – that personalized, tailored training and development is easily doable. It's time for L&D to lead by following its workforce into the future," they warned.

The following Canadian study illustrates what happens when workers are motivated to pull information without waiting for traditional training programmes.[33] Boutilier (2008) researched the learning of employees in a social services department involved in the implementation of new and highly problematic computer technology.

These social service employees were highly motivated to provide service to their clients. That motivation led them to engage in the creation of workarounds, non-standard procedures they developed to circumvent new software in order to meet their clients' needs. These workarounds were created primarily through individuals' trial-and-error learning, and were then shared, both informally and formally, through public official bulletins.

Boutilier stressed that the employees were not financially compensated for creating the workarounds and, indeed, felt at risk, because using the workarounds to accomplish their jobs frequently involved the violation of organizational policies.

Interestingly, other research has confirmed that employees will pull the information they want and need, no matter what the organizational or IT policies may be.

According to a Forrester Research report, 47 per cent of business technology users at North American and European companies report using one or more website(s) that are not sanctioned by their IT department to do part of their jobs. "We expect this number to grow as frustrated workers work around IT to self-provision technology," the report concluded.[34]

More evidence of how employees will go to great lengths to learn what they need to informally was revealed in a study of Canadian SMEs.[35] The study found that employees' informal learning included seeking out a coach or mentor, observing someone else at work, asking each other questions and trial and error. Their motivation was to solve problems as they arose on the job. They initiated cross-learning opportunities (learning about other employees' jobs) for two reasons: to be more effective in doing their own jobs and to give them the advantage when promotions or sick leave positions became available.

Their motivation to learn was indicated by the fact that they were engaged in informal learning even though it was not recognized in any systematic way. Cross-training was not offered to employees and was not formally recognized. Moreover, engaging in self-initiated cross-training could even be experienced as threatening to co-workers.

Employees continued to learn in spite of the dictum not to. That is, they found a way to do a job more effectively and efficiently, but kept the knowledge hidden from management because it was against policy. Since management did not value the employees' knowledge, these positive innovations were not shared upwards. Keeping knowledge to themselves also gave the workers more control over their workplaces, an increasing issue as technology allows management to monitor workers' activities minutely.

While learners prefer to take charge of their own learning, this does not mean that they enjoy solitary learning. Tough (1999) discovered that within each informal learning episode (where the primary motivation is to gain and retain certain knowledge and skill at a task or thing), the average learner interacts with an average of 10 people.[36] In fact, there may actually be more social interactions during informal learning episodes than there are in classrooms.

Most training is built on the pessimistic assumption that trainees are inadequate in some way. Training is the cure for what is broken. The consequences include:

- Negative reinforcement
- Unmotivated learners (who wants to accept that they are inadequate?)
- Learner disengagement, unrewarded curiosity, and spurned creativity because the training implies "My way or the highway"
- Training instead of learning (co-creation of knowledge)

- A focus on fixing the individual rather than optimising the team.

Instead of learning the answers to yesterday's problems, people need to learn how to deal with the unknown.

One of the key drivers for informal learning is the rate of change. More happens in a minute today than in one of your great-grandmother's minutes. Not only is more and more activity packed into every minute, the rate of change itself is increasing. Change itself is accelerating. The future is unpredictable. The traditional mode of training employees in isolation is becoming obsolete, or very close to being so. When training is done, it must be better integrated into the workspace and made more relevant to real-life needs.

Learning is like breathing: so much a part of our lives that we are unaware of it. Learning is that which enables you to participate successfully in life, at work and in the groups that matter to you. Informal learning is the unofficial, non-scheduled, impromptu way people learn to do their jobs. Learning is adaptation. Adapt or die: it is really about evolutionary pressure and survival through change.

Formal versus informal

With formal learning, employees are given the opportunity to acquire skills and knowledge that are defined and sanctioned by the organization. This gives employees the opportunity to spend paid time concentrating on learning defined essential knowledge and skills that allow them to be productive and flexible in their jobs. The skills and knowledge may also allow the employees to maintain their employability and to advance their careers.

The control of formal learning lies primarily in the hands of the organization. It may or may not have relevance to the individual, because the programme has been tailored to fit the needs of the organization. It is normally provided when the organization (or training provider) deems it suitable.

The timing is important, since the individual may or may not find the information useful or relevant at the time it is taught. By comparison, informal learning happens in real time, not weeks or months beforehand, as is often the case with formal learning. The learner is confronted by a situation in which he or she needs information and responds at that moment. It's called 'just in time' learning, whereas formal learning is more often 'just in case' learning – people are given information that they may need at some point in the future.

Training focuses on equipping individuals with the knowledge or skills they need to improve their performance to meet their current work conditions. It's essentially a short-term learning intervention, designed for immediate improvements in performance or to equip people with mandatory knowledge in areas such as food hygiene or health and safety. It's used to orientate new hires, qualify employees for special assignments or projects within the organization, or for cross-training.

Jay Cross says learning things in advance is "a losing game… Until the case arrives, the workers suspect that the subject matter won't be relevant. And when the case does come along, the knowledge acquired in advance is probably long forgotten. Knowledge, like muscle tissue, deteriorates when it's not used. But learning something at the moment of need couples learning to application, and has more lasting effects."[37]

Normally, formal training is highly structured and scheduled and tends to have a specific start and finish time and outcome. Informal learning is continual. It never stops because the world around the learner is constantly changing.

Formal learning begins with well-defined and measurable objectives and is deemed successful when evaluations show that those objectives have been achieved. For example, a person taking a certificate course might only be deemed successful if he or she passes the certification examination.

In contrast, informal learning often begins with vague goals and is deemed successful when workers themselves feel that they have benefitted from the learning. Outcomes may be tangible, such as new jobs and different work assignments, but they can also be intangible, such as the confidence that comes with knowledge and experience.

Informal learning occurs during organized work activities, such as meetings, working in teams, interaction with customers, supervision, mentoring, shift changes, peer-to-peer communication, cross-training, exploration, on the job training, documentation, execution of one's job, and site visits. In fact it can occur anytime, even away from the workplace. A scenario played out on a TV programme or in an interaction with a shop assistant could provide information that is retained and later used in the workplace.

Researchers found that assembly line workers and shift supervisors at Motorola were taking advantage of a 30-minute overlap in shift changes to update workers on the next shift on any problems that had occurred, as well as the probable causes and possible solutions.[38]

The control of informal learning rests primarily in the hands of the learner. The content is highly relevant and need-specific to the individual (but not necessarily the organization). What is learned tends to be used immediately on the job. Informal learning usually happens spontaneously, is unstructured and has no specific start or finish time. Informal learning might not even have a specific outcome. An example would be over-hearing something useful that was not even on the radar of the learner as a desirable bit of knowledge.

The 'Teaching Firm' research project was initiated in 1996 by the Education Development Centre Inc. (EDC) of Massachusetts.[39] It involved businesses, including Boeing, Ford Electronics, Siemens and Motorola, in six states in the US. The researchers found that critical learning skills are learned informally and that informal learning often takes precedence over formal learning. The project was based on the idea that the long-term employability and flexibility of American workers depends on employee's ability to learn on the job. It builds on the 1996 US Department of Labor's Bureau of Labor Statistics report which indicates that as much as 70 per cent of all workplace learning may be informal.

Their definition of informal learning is "learning in which the learning process is not determined by the organization".

Note that this definition distinguishes between the goals of learning and the process of learning. An organization may or may not have a goal for learning, yet learning is informal if it does not determine the process of learning. This definition allows for organizations to have explicit goals of increasing informal learning and creating the environment that will facilitate it.

The EDC report outlines how informal workplace learning is critical to a company's overall effectiveness and, ultimately, its ability to compete economically in a rapidly changing and increasingly demanding global marketplace.

This 1996 study was the first to use a large body of empirical findings (over 1,000 participants) describing informal workplace learning. As a whole, the study presents compelling evidence that informal learning is the fundamental way that workers develop competence and acquire new skills and information.

Having said that, the report also goes on to say that employees develop skills and knowledge through a combination of both formal and informal learning opportunities. Informal learning is ubiquitous and fulfils many learning needs; however, when both informal and formal learning occur, employees have richer opportunities for development. Formal and informal learning exist along a continuum, rather than being two dichotomous processes.

Note the date of this study – 1996. This is prior to any significant impact of the internet on the workplace. Even email was in its infancy. The same research today would almost certainly show informal learning as being even more important in the daily workplace, given the way employees now access information online from their PCs or mobile devices.

The report concluded that informal workplace learning occurs in the course of work activities and includes:

- Acquisition and application of skills and knowledge
- Movement along the continuum from inexperience to confidence
- Maturity and expertise with regard to specific tasks, skills and knowledge.

Employees also develop essential knowledge and skills around other facets of the workplace, including:

- Intrapersonal: problem solving, creativity, coping with stress and dealing with novel situations

- Interpersonal: interacting, cooperating, and sharing skills and information with other employees
- Culture: understanding acceptable behaviour and the norms that are culturally rewarded and lead to career advancement.

Certain key factors determine how much informal learning occurs in the workplace, as well as how much the individual employee is motivated to learn. These factors include

- External industry/economic factors, such as the level of competition
- How HR policies and practices, as experienced by workers, match against the formal policies and practices
- Social and environmental factors, such as physical work conditions and social norms
- Personal characteristics and developmental needs of individual employees within the organization.

Another finding of the report is that informal learning is extremely context sensitive and that the same activities in different contexts will yield different informal learning results. A consequence of this is that the context relating to informal learning within an organization needs to be analysed to gain an understanding of how to intervene to increase informal learning. There is no 'one size fits all' solution, although it is clear that informal learning is productive for both the company and its workers when a company's culture and practices fully support informal learning. The Teaching Firm research consistently demonstrates the importance of providing a productive environment for informal learning.

The following table sets out the main differences between formal and informal learning in the workplace.

In the ASTD/i4cp study, 'Tapping the potential of informal learning', most respondents said informal learning enhances performance to at least a moderate extent and 46 per cent of all respondents said it improves employee performance to a high or very high extent. But these responses are not the only indicators as to why managers should devote attention to informal learning. The study also found a significant, positive correlation between the degree to which informal learning occurs in organizations and their reported market performance.

Formal learning	Informal learning
Typically provided by a training department	Resulting from daily life activities related to work, family or leisure
Structured in terms of learning objectives, learning time or learning support	Not structured (flexible) in terms of learning objectives, learning time or learning support
Leads to certification	Typically does not lead to certification
Intentional	May be intentional, but in most cases is non-intentional (incidental/random)

Table 1: Formal versus informal learning (European Commission 2001)

Informal learning can, however, be inefficient and time-consuming and the information may not always be accurate. A CIO Magazine survey found that workers spent more than seven hours a week searching for information. An IDC Information Worker Survey in April 2003 found that 15 to 30 per cent of work time is spent actively seeking information.

Informal learning presents a number of other challenges, including workers learning material incorrectly when studying on their own, choosing to finish studying before they have actually mastered the content, lacking the motivation to continue learning, and receiving no acknowledgment for their studies.

How informal learning happens in the workplace

Allen Tough, a Professor Emeritus at the University of Toronto, researched adults' successful efforts to learn and change and, in particular, the 70 per cent that is self-guided, without relying much on professionals or institutions (informal learning). During his research, he discovered that people spend an average of 15 hours per week learning on their own.[40]

In the late 1970s, Patrick Penland, a professor at the University of Pittsburgh, performed a survey, part of which focused on why learners prefer to learn on their own, rather than in a class or course.[41] The main reasons, in ranking order, were:

- I want to set my own learning pace
- I want to use my own style of learning
- I want to keep the learning strategy flexible and easy to change
- I want to put my own structure on the learning project
- I didn't know of any class that taught what I wanted to know
- I wanted to learn this right away and couldn't wait until a class might start
- I had no time to engage in a group learning programme
- I don't like a formal classroom situation with a teacher
- I don't have enough money for a course or class
- Transportation to a class is too hard or expensive.

Interestingly, it shows that the main reason learners like informal learning is not that they lack resources or hate attending formal classes, but that they prefer being in charge of their own learning.

From that list, it's possible to identify eight characteristics that impact most informal learning episodes:

1. It's self-paced.
2. It's personalized.
3. It's tactical.
4. It provides empowerment.
5. It's complex.
6. It's just-in-time.
7. It's flexible.
8. It's casual.

In 2000 and 2001, Graham Cheetham and Geoff Chivers surveyed practitioners in six professions to determine which out of 10 types of informal learning or experiences helped them to become fully competent.[42] Respondents were able to choose more than one type of informal learning.

On the job learning was the most popular (with an average 4.2 rating out of 5), followed by working alongside more experienced colleagues (rated 3.9 out of 5), working as part of a team (rated 3.7 out of 5), self-analysis or reflection (rated 3.6 out of 5), learning from clients, patients or customers (rated 3.5 out of 5), networking with others doing similar work (rated 3.4 out of 5), learning through teaching or training others (rated 3.1 out of 5), support from a mentor (rated 3.2 out of 5) and use of a role model (rated 2.6 out of 5).

Theorists in the field of work-related informal learning, Marsick and Watkins, identified the following informal learning activities:[43]

- Task accomplishment
- Trial and error
- Self-directed learning
- Networking
- Coaching
- Mentoring
- Performance planning.

More recent surveys[44] in Canada and the USA expanded the list of self-directed learning methods to include such activities as:

- Seeking advice from someone knowledgeable
- Using the internet or other software
- Observing someone performing a task
- Consulting books or manuals
- Teaching oneself how to do tasks differently
- Self-paced study using books or video tapes
- Self-paced study using computers
- Attending conferences, fairs or conventions
- Reading manuals, reference material or professional journals or magazines
- Learning through assignments in different parts of an organization
- Attending lectures, seminars or special talks
- Using video, television or tapes to learn
- Getting help from others.

Type of learning	Format	Method of delivery
Formal (structured learning in which a curriculum is required)	Live/interactive (requires interaction between individuals)	Classroom learning, virtual classroom
Formal (structured learning in which a curriculum is required)	Just-in-time/self-paced (learning without direct interaction with another individual)	Self-study guides, distance learning, and computer, web, video or audio based training
Informal (learning without the help of a structured curriculum)	Live/interactive learning that requires interaction between individuals	A help desk, a coaching or mentoring session, collaboration, communities of practice, presentations, virtual knowledge sharing, desk-side support
Informal (learning without the help of a structured curriculum)	Just-in-time/ self-paced (this is learning without direct interaction with another individual)	Publications, reference guides, job aides, electronic performance support systems, or online self help

Table 2: The different delivery methods of formal and informal learning

Characteristics of informal learning

How do you know when someone is learning informally?

The short answer is that they are aware – aware of themselves and their surroundings. This means they are processing information and making new neural connections. Some would even say new connections are made while we are asleep and dreaming. Informal learning is indeed ubiquitous, but what does it look like in a work context?

The following list will help you and your department to recognize it.

Informal learning happens just-in-time

Informal learning is 'just-in-time' – it'll usually happen right when the learner can put the knowledge or skills to immediate use. For example, an employee needs to find out how to use the database and asks his colleague in the next cubicle. He didn't have to attend a workshop or training course to find the information.

Informal learning happens in context

Informal learning usually happens in context – 'on-the-job'. A manager in the sales department discusses preparing sales reports with two of her employees. They all meet in her office within the department so they can look at her computer screen to see exactly how it's done.

Informal learning is part of a learning continuum

Some early informal learning proponents put forth the idea that informal learning was the opposite of formal learning, but they have now to come to see that both are part of a learning continuum.

Formal and informal learning are both learning, and both involve building new neural connections in the brain and adapting to new conditions.

At one end is the regimented approach – and I use that word on purpose. It was the military that started training people in groups to be 'clones', to be able all to do the same thing in the same way. Think back to the Roman military machine, which focused on a standardization of infantry manoeuvres that enabled it to conquer the known world. Someone decided what they should all be able to do, and then devised training to ensure that happened. Much later, as the scale of industry and businesses grew, so did the need for significant numbers of people to acquire identical skills. The military approach to group training was the obvious answer. Alongside this, the education system also grew and this too used an approach where experts decided what needed to be learned, and then devised training to teach it.

Formal learning is often the primary need of novices in a field. Formal training can enable them to rapidly build a framework of knowledge which then allows the information from subsequent informal learning in that area to be retained.

At the other end of the continuum is informal learning. Here, there is no fixed outcome or curriculum, or the opportunity to graduate with a grade and a certificate. Informal learning will often better suit more experienced people who have already established a base of knowledge in an area. They just want to learn whatever they need at the time to fill in the gaps that enable them to accomplish their tasks.

Informal learning cannot and should not be separated from formal learning, according to a research report written by Margaret Dale and John Bell.[45] "Both are needed and fit together. Informal learning supports and is supported by formal learning. Informal learning does not replace formal learning; it complements it and has some drawbacks."

The following example illustrates how elements of both informal and formal learning blend together. Writing in the 'Training Journal', Vincent Belliveau, General Manager of Europe, Middle East and Africa at integrated learning and talent management software and services provider, Cornerstone OnDemand, explained how the London Business School is using technology as a form of online introduction to its many thousands of new executive students.[46]

The London Business School is one of the top ten global business schools, with an executive education team that serves more than 7,400 executives on a variety of open and custom programmes each year.

Many of its students are busy executives who have not engaged in formal education or training for some time, so having an online introduction to the subject matter in advance helps maximize the impact of classroom-based learning. In addition, faculty and programme directors need to identify, understand and assess each participant's needs so the programme – particularly the coaching element – will generate real improvements in their skills and abilities.

Moreover, participants come from a wide range of countries, making it difficult to assess their needs by telephone. The executive education team identified that online collaboration tools could help participants, faculty and programme directors to interact and prepare before the start of a programme, and also noted demand (particularly from younger executives) for social networking functionality to enrich the learning and networking experience.

When informal learning is integrated with formal learning, it produces a significantly stronger retention of learning than would be possible through either type of learning on its own.

To be effective, training needs to be followed up and applied on the job, but research has shown there's too little follow-up. An ASTD study in 2006 found that 70 per cent of training failure happens after the formal training finishes, with only 10 per cent of training failure attributed to actual learning events.[47] The transfer of learning is often given low priority and poorly followed-up. Moreover, there are too few opportunities for learners to use what they've learnt.

If people aren't given the opportunity to review and use what they have learnt, they quickly forget the information.

One of the first people to study the process of forgetting was the German psychologist Hermann Ebbinghaus. He conducted an experiment in which he memorized lists of three-letter nonsense words and then tracked how quickly he forgot the words at different time intervals, ranging from 20 minutes to 31 days.

Ebbinghaus' results revealed a relationship between the forgetting of learned information and the passage of time. He found that a good part of what a person forgets takes place within 20 minutes of the initial learning. Within one hour, a person forgets nearly half of what was originally learned. After 24 hours, almost two-thirds of the previously-learned material is forgotten. These results are known as the 'Ebbinghaus forgetting curve'.

He discovered that it is much harder to retain information that has no meaning for the learner. He also showed that re-learning material is easier than the initial learning and that it takes longer to forget material the second time.

Finally, he showed that a person will have greater success with learning if the studying is spread out over time, rather than fitted into a single session.

Formal training can be used to support informal learning

Formal training can provide employers with a way to support informal learning. Mentors can work with employees taking formal courses and help them understand how they can integrate the content into their daily work, for example.

The Central Intelligence Agency (CIA) launched a wiki, Intellipedia, in 2006 to enable its agents around the world to share knowledge, tips and ideas with each other. They offer employees training programmes to teach them how to make the best use of informal learning opportunities such as this.

The organization has developed training programmes that help analysts integrate social software tools into their daily work habits. These classes generally focus on the use of Intellipedia to capture and manage knowledge, but they also incorporate the use of the other social software tools. These include blogs, RSS and social bookmarking. The courses stress immersion in the tools and instructors encourage participants to work on a specific project in Intellipedia.

Informal learning can support formal training

A lot of informal learning takes place in the small spaces between formal learning episodes – "between the cracks," according to Bob Hoffman, author of *Informal Learning: Tips, Tools and Intelligence for Trainers*.[48] "People often want more discussion than they get in many formal workshops, and they tend to take advantage of lunch and refreshment breaks – not to mention carpooling to and from the workshop – to satisfy that desire."

These discussions help people to:

- Consider other perspectives
- Compare the theory they're getting in the workshop to the personal experiences they and others have had
- Share their understanding to identify gaps in their knowledge and raise new questions
- Process the content of whatever formal instruction they're getting.

Common wisdom, says Hoffman, has it that socializing at professional conferences is at least as valuable as attending formal presentations and workshops. "In addition to strengthening and making new professional contacts, people talk about what they're learning. Formal instruction is often designed with too much information presentation and not enough processing and practice. The interstices provide that valuable learning space."

Another way that informal learning can support formal training is when, after completing a formal training course or programme, employees decide either to find the answer to a question that arose, but wasn't addressed during the course or programme, or to explore the topic in more detail.

Nowadays, formal courses may use wikis and forums to develop and discuss ideas.

Executive and management support plays a critical role

For informal learning to succeed, employees must believe they have the support of executives and managers in their learning efforts. That support means employers:

- Allow employees to learn during work time
- Allow mistakes to be made during the learning process
- Make it clear that mistakes are part of any learning process
- Recognize and acknowledge informal learning efforts
- Act as informal learning role models by embracing and using it themselves.

The commitment of the manager and the skills of those supporting the learning environment are prerequisites to successful informal learning.

Informal learning is ubiquitous

One of the most important things to remember about informal learning is that it is present in all workplace environments and day-to-day activities. It is the essential way in which individuals grow with the ever-changing needs of the business environment, and their lives. People will always be learning in the workplace; people cannot not learn. The question, of course, is what are they learning and how much are they learning?

Informal learners access more than one resource to learn

Informal learners usually rely on several resources to learn (published materials, case studies, activities, access to experiences, coaching, advice, conversations and so on), so to promote informal learning in your organization, you need to develop, acquire and offer those resources. This isn't always easy, because while some explicit content (organizational structures, responsibilities, processes, job descriptions and so on) may already exist, some resources may be undocumented (they may reside in the minds of subject matter experts in your organization, for example).

Once the resources are available, L&D professionals need to make employees aware that they exist and encourage them to access them. It's important that L&D makes it easy for employees to locate and access such resources. They also need to ensure that the material is accurate, relevant and easy to use.

Workers need to be encouraged to participate in discussions about the material and share their knowledge and insights with others in the organization. They also need to be encouraged to seek out opportunities to apply the knowledge they've learnt.

Informal learners follow their own interests

Informal learners tend to explore areas they find most interesting, which may not always serve the organization's learning agenda. They will learn or find out about things that enable them to participate effectively in whatever motivates them at the time. This may be a current problem they want to solve, or it may be a new project they want to be involved in because it is exciting and aligns with their values.

Informal learners may lack learning skills

Many informal learners may also lack learning skills, such as the ability to find the material they want, to learn from what they find, and then to transfer that to the job. They may find it hard to locate and discern valuable content from the mass of available knowledge.

They may find it difficult to unlearn information that is getting in the way of new information. Their beliefs may also interfere with how they approach information or with what they discover.

That's why it's important for L&D professionals to address their employees' ability to find information, assess the quality of that information and recognize when what they've previously learnt or believed is interfering with their new learning.

One of the challenges of informal learning is that, because it doesn't have an official beginning or an official ending, it is hard to determine whether an employee has finished a learning effort. This makes it very difficult for L&D professionals to determine whether workers have learned the material correctly and, if necessary, what would motivate them to complete a particular learning endeavour.

Informal learning can be inefficient and inaccurate

There's a risk that if employees can't find the information they need from a business-sanctioned knowledge source, they will look for what they need externally. A lack of efficiency can result when external sources are used. For example, the interaction might not be captured and, consequently, the employee or peers might not be able to be rediscover the information. There is also no way to ensure the information that is obtained is relevant or reliable. The process could result in less than best practice being implemented, and that practice could spread as informal learners share their knowledge with others.

Informal learning often happens socially

Informal learning often takes place through collaboration on work teams. People learn from others who are not in their immediate work environment, using informal networks. These networks often involve people in and out of the immediate work environment – and inside and outside the organization – and are valuable sources of news, technical content, advice and insights.

The networks might be made up of existing colleagues, former colleagues (both inside and outside the current organization), former classmates, members of professional organizations and bloggers, as well as members of social media networks, such as Twitter, LinkedIn Groups and Facebook, among others.

If someone has a question about a specific problem or issue and can access an expert on that issue through their personal network, they may be able to receive a speedy response. This saves the organization time and money.

In 2008, Mitchell, Frazzee, Panitch, Luciani and Bowan conducted a survey of bank employees involved in implementing a new software system for financial services. They found that employees were motivated to learn informally because the time allotted to use more formal, self-directed training materials, such as computer-based training software, was inadequate. In order to perform their day-to-day tasks and cope with the stress of the new system, the workers had to learn informally from each other.

Although the employer had introduced computer-based self-study materials, the employees organized informal learning groups to help each other master the formalized training materials. They continued to use other informal learning activities, such as asking each other for help, seeking out a coach or mentor, or self-organized cross-training. Furthermore, they reported a strong preference for informal learning activities over more formalized training.

The challenge of evaluating informal learning

Using existing L&D measures to evaluate informal learning presents challenges. Traditionally, trainers and developers measure the effectiveness of a learning programme with an evaluation tool, such as David Kirkpatrick's chain reaction model. This is based on the principle that there are five distinct stages of learning and change that can be measured to gauge the impact of the learning programme.

The five chain reaction stages are: training, which leads to reaction, which leads to learning, which leads to changes in job behaviour, which leads to change in the organization.

The evaluation begins with a formative look at the processes used on the programme, moving on to the measurements of reactions (how trainees felt about the programme and how they responded to aspects of it). These reactions lead to learning, measured against learning outcomes set for the programme.

Evaluators may try to assess whether there were any unintended learning outcomes. The learning should result in individuals changing their behaviour in the workplace (in line with the learning outcomes), which will ultimately lead to changes in organizational performance.

But even as a measurement tool for formal training, the chain reaction model is limited. "In practice, the chain often breaks down when attempts are made to link learning outcomes achieved on the course to the effects on job behaviours and evaluation is then limited to an assessment of reactions through an end-of-course questionnaire and some testing of learning outcomes which can be built into the programme," according to Jeff Gold and his co-editors of the *Gower Handbook of Leadership and Management Development*.[49]

The reason is that it is very difficult to measure learning transfer, seen when learners attempt to apply what they've learned in a training room in their normal work environment. Trying to measure the final step in the chain reaction evaluation process – organizational impact – is the most problematic of all, they say.

"The problem lies in trying to disentangle and then reconnect individual learning and organizational performance in a sterile 'cause and effect' way rather than acknowledging that a wide range of factors impact on how organizations perform and trying to understand which of these can be affected by management development initiatives."

Although it is possible to apply a chain reaction approach to person-centred learning, it is unlikely to produce helpful results.

Kirkpatrick's framework assumes that learning happens in formally defined events that have well-defined objectives and are intended to address a business need. But none of these criteria necessarily apply to informal learning for the workplace. Much of informal learning results from a process in which several experiences – some planned, many unplanned – result in changes in behaviour, knowledge, beliefs or attitudes. Some of the changes are visible and easily identified; others are unconscious, so uncovering them requires extensive work.

Formal learning in a training context is primarily rooted in behaviourism (which defines learning as a change in behaviour), while informal learning is rooted in constructivism, which characterizes learning, not as a change in behaviour, but as changes in knowledge, beliefs and attitudes – most of which cannot be observed or measured, but some of which are reflected in new skills and processes.

Behaviourism is based on a belief that knowledge is fixed and is consistent across individuals. The design of formal learning programmes allows evaluators to identify and measure the behaviours that change as a result of the learning. Constructivism suggests that knowledge is constructed through experience and influenced by interaction with other people. Each person has a unique collection of experiences and knowledge. Constructivism often portrays learning as a process or journey. This makes it difficult to transfer many of the core practices of L&D professionals (writing objectives, offering courses, conducting tests and evaluations) into a constructivist approach.

Informal learning can be cost-effective

With informal learning, there's no need for expensive training programmes or for employees to take time away from the office – people learn wherever they are. By empowering people to publish their expertise and learn from each other, you can cut spending on content development, external content and formal training.

Learners can provide immediate feedback on content

The fact that the social and mobile web offers small chunks of content enables learners to select for quality and relevance. Learners who self-select their curriculum can instantly provide feedback if a piece of content is helpful or unappealing, signalling in real time the knowledge that resonates and makes a difference for them, and by implication their organization.

Informal learners don't always realize they're learning

Participants often do not perceive themselves to be 'learning', particularly when this takes place in an unstructured setting. This perception is an important factor in overcoming resistance to participation. It is also an important factor when surveying people about learning. They will say they are not learning, when in fact they are doing so without realizing it. Much of this is down to how people have been trained by our education system to think of learning as a formal event, where an expert tells them the right way to do something.

Informal learning can happen at every stage of employment.

Informal learning occurs at every level of employment, from job entry and basic skill acquisition, through to ongoing development of people in senior and experienced roles. One of the most valuable skills to learn is the skill of continuous learning.

Informal learning usually occurs in small chunks

Unlike formal learning events, which can last from a few hours to a few days, informal learning events are usually completed in minutes or, at most, a few hours. The information is obtained in a more organic, just-in-time fashion. What's more, because the learner is getting the information in small chunks, interspersed with periods of practice and rest, he or she will be likely to store more of it in long-term memory than if they were sitting through an intensive training session.

Informal learning is limited in scope

An informal learning occurrence is limited in scope and might involve a specific skill or a small bit of knowledge, rather than an extended, formal training session or course.

Informal learning is individualized

Informal learning is individualized to meet specific needs. One employee might ask his or her predecessor, for example, to show him how to put together a monthly sales report and then take the opportunity to find out how to deal with the finance department.

It is also individualized in the sense that what is learnt builds directly on the learner's prior knowledge. For example, an employee might want information that is quite specialized and for which there is unlikely to be a formal training programme, since it's likely to be something that few others in the organization need. However, she needs that information to do a specific part of her job. She thinks of someone within the organization who has that information and gets in contact with that person. What she needs to know won't take long to obtain because she already has a level of expertise in that area.

Informal learning in its different guises

Informal learning takes place in a variety of guises in the workplace. These include what Marcia L. Conner calls accidental, intentional, non-formal and social learning.

Accidental learning

Accidental learning takes place as a result of engaging in everyday activities, without expectations or intentions on the part of either the learner or the organization. Examples of accidental learning include a lunchtime conversation that reveals organizational culture or a casual chat about a software feature.

Intentional learning

In the case of intentional learning, individuals define their own learning outcomes, choose learning strategies to accomplish those outcomes and pursue those at their own pace. Examples of intentional learning include finding a good tutorial and sitting down with a new piece of software, or checking out a book on hiring practices.

Non-formal learning

In the context of the workplace, non-formal learning really means an otherwise formal activity – a course or a workshop, for example – that isn't sponsored or sanctioned by the organization. An example would be when an administrative assistant finds and completes an online course in a spread sheet application.

Social learning

Social learning covers all those instances in which people learn from others, in so-called 'communities of practice'. Examples include a new hire shadowing an experienced salesperson, or an engineer seeking advice from a user group or a developer's forum.

Why the interest in informal learning?

One of the biggest factors is the growing awareness of the frequency and importance of informal learning in the working lives of most adults. The first large-scale study of informal learning in the workplace was done in 1996 and fully published in 1998.[50] Most studies are far more recent and they have built up an overwhelming store of evidence that informal learning is a vital component of organizational effectiveness.

There are also other interacting causes and sources for the interest: for example, shrinking L&D budgets have forced people to revisit the whole question of learning within the workplace, how it happens and how they can improve upon it. So the current financial climate is a major factor, because it has forced companies to look for low-cost and highly-effective learning opportunities. With cutbacks in training and resources, employees themselves have in many cases taken responsibility for their own learning.

It is taken as read that learning itself is critical to success and this was succinctly put by Jake Reynolds: "Learning leads to adaptations in the behaviour of employees that, if properly aligned with group and corporate goals, will allow the organization to deliver greater value to stakeholders".

If learning is important, and a lot of it is happening informally, then people want to know just how much learning is informal, and what that means in practice.

A 2009 Conference Board of Canada study reported that 56 per cent of work-related learning occurred in informal contexts.[51] Jay Cross and others suggest this percentage is closer to 80.[52] In 1998 and 2004, David Livingstone and his colleagues at OISE (Ontario Institute for Studies in Education) conducted national surveys focused on adults' informal learning and work.[53] These surveys indicated high rates of participation in work-related informal learning.

The arrival in the workplace of those born towards the end of the last century – the 'Millennials' – is another contributing factor. They are impatient, energetic and have little time for hierarchy. They are the first to have grown up using technology, both at work and at home. Being used to the internet and social media, they expect to be able to access information almost instantly, in a way quite unlike that of the working generations that preceded them: the baby boomers, generation X and the traditionalists. By 2015, Millennials will make up the most significant part of the workforce.

Their approach to learning has three key characteristics: it is naturally social, it is non-hierarchical and it is impatient. That impatience means they are generally very clear about what they want to know and very clear about how they want to learn it. They want to learn it immediately, and without any extraneous information. They are unlikely to want to sit through a traditional training course. They will instead seek out what they want when they want it, reference it and, probably, share it.

Growing dissatisfaction with the effectiveness of the formal education system and off-the-job training has also been a factor in the emergence of on-the-job informal learning as a field of interest.

The quality and cost of classroom courses has led to increased frustration with formal learning. Studies have shown that many training courses fail to meet the needs of organizations or learners. There's also the fact that courses are often not available when learners need the content. When the courses are available, employees have to take time away from the office, which many don't like (fearing their desks will be piled high with additional work by the time they get back). And their managers often don't like the time they are away from their desks, due to short-term operational issues.

Traditional methods of training have shown rapid knowledge loss, says Tom Hoglund, a senior executive who runs the collaboration and knowledge management practice on a global basis for the consulting firm, Accenture.[54] For example, he notes that 60 per cent of material can be forgotten 24 hours after a formal class is given.

Informal learning fits the context of today's knowledge-on-the-go world, where information is best processed in small information bites, he says. "It's a perfect storm of pressures from the budget and newer generations of workers, and companies that have had success with informal learning are seeing good results."

Cost is another factor. It is expensive hiring training facilities and trainers and there is a short-term loss in productivity, because employees are not doing work that is immediately productive.

Employers are turning to informal training methods to help reduce learning and development costs, according to research by XpertHR. Two-thirds of the organizations taking part in their survey have taken steps to cut back on training expenditure in the past year, and among these, 80 per cent have turned to informal learning as a cost-cutting measure.

Along with the reduced use of external providers, informal learning methods, such as work-shadowing, secondments, mentoring and social networking, are considered by the HR professionals taking part to be the most effective ways to reduce expenditure.

Other examples of measures taken to reduce outlay on training include:

- More cross-organizational collaboration
- Increased involvement of managers in the delivery of training
- More rigorous training needs analysis against business strategy.

Many training departments are not keeping up with the changes in technologies and the social networked world we now live in. And those changes are accelerating. Many courses are already out of date as the pilot is delivered. Much of what workers need to learn is a moving target, which makes learning in advance impractical. Life as we knew it in the golden days of training is gone. Rapid change in the workplace makes ongoing informal learning critical.

The web has transformed informal learning, offering over a billion people ready access to information and ideas on a vast array of topics. Google and other search engines are now the biggest learning providers on the planet. They answer over two billion searches per day for the 33 per cent of the world's population who are online.

The rapid growth of Web 2.0 has made it possible for individuals and organizations to have readily-accessible and highly-interactive information networks. Corporations that understand the value of knowledge sharing, teamwork, informal learning and joint problem-solving are investing heavily in collaboration technology and are reaping the early rewards. Furthermore, informal learning is highly visible in the form of recorded interchanges taking place in wikis, blogs and other interactive websites.

A recent report from McKinsey Global Institute (MGI) estimates that social technologies could potentially contribute between $900 billion and $1.3 trillion in annual value in just four industry sectors.[55] And whereas most business use of social networking so far has been external-facing, the MGI report finds that two-thirds of that potential value lies inside the company. It estimates that the use of social tools to enhance communications, knowledge sharing and collaboration can enhance the productivity of high-skill knowledge workers by 20 to 25 per cent.

We have been social learning experts since we sat around fires in our long-forgotten caves. The new social connection technologies have simply expanded the numbers of people with whom we can connect, and have thus supercharged our ability to connect, have conversations, listen to stories and make sense of what we discuss. Technology has globalized and accelerated our social experience.

The emergence of social media has given individuals and teams the tools to support their own learning and performance needs much more easily and powerfully themselves. It is now L&D's job to support this and the new ways that people are learning.

Alongside the growth of social media technologies are new programmes that allow non-technical people to prepare and post online information in various formats, from e-learning to wikis and blogs. Subject matter experts can get templates from learning content management systems to guide them through the process of providing material on a given subject so that it contains all of the information that workers need.

There is now an explosion of information available, and with the advent of mobile data and smartphones, it is available almost anywhere.

A report by Claire Schooley of Forrester Research[56] highlights three trends that have made it necessary for companies to adopt new informal learning practices at corporations:

1. Information overload in the workplace.
2. The immediacy with which information is desired.
3. The work style of the Millennial generation (for example, the desire to drive one's learning, rather than being a passive recipient of knowledge).

Schooley emphasizes that the idea behind all of these informal methods is user-initiated learning, whether it be through harnessing social networks, blended learning solutions, or creating employee knowledge centres for just-in-time learning. She also sees value in aligning learning with whatever is going on in the company, which includes having senior executives encouraging young employees to directly contribute to the learning culture.

Another trend, identified by Saul Carliner, is towards increasingly dynamic knowledge-based work assignments.[57] This stems from computerization. Since computers provide decision-makers with information more quickly, they have helped organizations develop sophisticated business strategies that allow them to better target their activities and respond faster to external events. This, in turn, has resulted in greater flexibility of work assignments.

This flexibility takes many forms, he says. One is more flexible work teams that bring together people with the expertise needed on a particular project, and then disband when workers have completed their project. Another is shorter product development cycles.

It means organizations expect their employees to become more productive more quickly. Employees need to develop knowledge and skills as fast as possible, but it's not always possible for L&D to create the programmes when they need them.

This, says Carliner, ushers in the need for informal learning programmes.

Chapter 4

Informal learning in practice

"Knowledge sharing is the basis of everything. Share knowledge with reckless abandon."

Tim Sanders, Chief Solutions Officer at Yahoo

By now, you may be thinking that informal learning makes sense in theory, but perhaps you're wondering what it looks like in practice. How will you recognize it in your organization? The following examples illustrate how informal learning takes place in companies, private and public, large and small, around the world. The examples are in no specific order in the sense that there is a priority or 'best' way to do informal learning. As stated earlier, context is critical, and hence what works well in one organization may not work so well in another with a different culture, different workforce demographics, different access to technology and so on.

As you read through, think how the example or method could be integrated into your organization. Notice how you personally react to the example as something that feels right or makes sense to you and be aware that someone else reading it could be reacting differently. This is one of the real challenges of encouraging informal learning in that it is so personal to the learner. You will always need a Smörgåsbord approach for informal learning initiatives, rather than a set menu.

Examples

The following examples include some headings in an attempt to separate out different informal learning methods. Be aware, however, that while the headings make initial reading easier, informal learning does not in practice divide up into separate methods quite so easily, and these methods certainly don't fit nicely under simple headings. Specific informal learning methods can rarely be implemented in isolation. Successful implementation of informal learning involves lots of methods, with the learners choosing which combination of them is useful at any particular time.

Some of the following examples include referenced case studies, and some include stories which are apocryphal, or a pastiche of real-life examples that illustrate the point, and will hopefully generate ideas for you to use.

On-the-job training

At a large manufacturing company, when new employees received on the job training, informal learning practices included a certain amount of trial and error on the job, plus time to observe, ask questions, share information, read and network. These factors played a key role in a new employee's orientation to the pragmatics of the job.

New employees also stated that the allowed reflection time gave them opportunities to come up with questions that were not immediately apparent.

It also gave them time to ask questions about the company's culture, including the hierarchy, internal politics, corporate values and accepted methods of behaviour and communication. Acculturation occurred more frequently through informal training techniques, since employee expectations of what they needed to know are rarely explicit and therefore much more difficult to learn through formal methods.

At this same company, researchers observed one trainer who was particularly good at training – a former Sunday school teacher, who had years of experience training new employees, and who was motivated and patient with trainees' initial mistakes. Since the job required learning a complex task, he would also closely observe a trainee over a long period of time, as his work station was located nearby. This gave the trainer the opportunity to provide constant, real-time feedback.

The trainer would eventually report to the first-line supervisor that the trainee was ready to work independently, but with an occasional check from him. Once the on-the-job training was considered completed, the trainer would announce in the weekly team meeting that the trainee had completed the practice session. The team would congratulate the trainee with a certificate of achievement. Soon afterwards, the trainee would be observed slowly gaining the confidence to work on his own, still asking his trainer questions, but eventually working with him as a peer.

At Avis Budget Group (the parent organization of Avis Rent A Car and Budget Rent A Car), new hires are guided through a list of structured experiences – including cleaning a car and operating a filling station island safely – before they receive any formal training. The Marriott hotel group has its managers teach employees how to clean rooms and serve customers in much the same way.

Bottom-up learning

As part of his efforts to ensure the quality of the millions of lattes and cappuccinos Starbucks serves, Starbucks' CEO Howard Schultz forbade what had become the common practice of re-steaming milk. This meant baristas were pouring millions of pints of valuable milk down the drain. Once economic pressures began to bite, somebody at corporate headquarters finally embraced a store manager's solution: put etched lines in the steaming pitchers so that the baristas would know how much milk to use for each size of a specific drink. Before, they just guessed.[58]

In another example, Nokia decided to encourage its employees to critique the company. It set up online environments, called BlogHub and Sphere, specifically to encourage and capture employee rants on what they thought needed changing – from its purchasing practices to how its software works.

The push-backs and critiques now flow right into company R&D. Rapid changes in its touch screens, keyboards and specialized local services for customers all have their origins in employee rants.

Mobile learning

Mobile learning (also known as m-learning) is personalized and involves accessing information through a mobile electronic device. It can be done on a wide range of such devices, including mobile phones, smartphones, personal digital assistants, laptops and netbooks, electronic tablet devices, MP3 players, portable navigation devices, digital cameras, portable gaming devices, and USB storage devices.

It facilitates speedy communication, is portable and convenient, creates active learning experiences, and usually allows for learning connectivity at any time and in any location.

Mobile devices can deliver the right information to enable people to be capable in the moment to tackle the immediate task they have in front of them. Learners are more likely to retain what they learn via a mobile device, because it is relevant information, delivered at the moment they need it, and then used immediately in context.

Many of the learners already possess mobile learning devices, and often prefer to use their own rather than a cheaper alternative supplied by their employer. There is a growing trend in workplaces to BYOD or Bring Your Own Device.

The learning opportunities available via mobile devices include how-to videos, interactive tutorials, frequently asked questions, and searchable help sections. Information can also be gathered from the internet via the use of feeds, such as Egress, Bloglines Mobile, Avant Reader, FeederReader, Google Reader Mobile, NewsBreak, Litefeeds and Smartfeed. Digital media channels, such as iTunes and YouTube, are great resources for group mobile learning.

One of the most beneficial aspects of mobile learning software is that it allows individuals to collaborate at the moment of need with others who are not in close geographic proximity.

Because mobile learning depends largely on the employee's ability to actively pursue learning, the power has to shift from the managers and instructors to the learners themselves. This will require encouragement of self-discipline and self-direction within employees.

This is less of an issue where the mobile device is used for just-in-time support, where the worker can access information they need to carry out their immediate task. For this kind of support, the organization needs to allow its knowledge management system and other knowledge resources to be accessible via mobile devices.

As an example, one of the world's largest fashion glasses manufacturers is using highly interactive and multimedia-rich mobile learning to teach its laboratory assistants how to use different machines to polish and finish lenses.[59]

Mobile learning in action – an example

In another example, a pilot scheme tested the use of game consoles in learning. We have quoted extensively from this case study by IRSS with their permission, because it offers such rich pickings. Keith Quinn, a Senior Education and Workplace Development Adviser with Scottish Social Services Council, described how he piloted a learning module which used the Sony PlayStation Portable (PSP) console to deliver on-the-spot training in the workplace.[60]

"We know that it is becoming increasingly difficult to release staff for learning, mainly because the workforce isn't available to backfill any more, but also because there are legal minimums that people need to meet in terms of keeping people engaged in service delivery, when it comes to registration and regulation of service. So some of the core issues we wanted to address were the logistics of learning: this whole thing about transporting people to a central location to learn and then transporting them back.

"When we spoke to employers, they were saying to us that costs, in real terms, were £200 per day per employee. And even if organizations are delivering the minimum that we require in terms of ongoing registration needs, which is 15 days over three years, that amounts to about £1,000 per employee. So over the entire workforce, that is £198,000,000 spent just on in-service training. If 20 per cent of that moved to e-learning, or e-learning delivered on mobile devices in the workplace, that is a saving of £39,500,000, and it also addresses the thing about taking people out of the workplace in order to learn.

"And we did a research project on the back of this which kind of looked at how these logistics actually played out in the real world.

"In terms of the research project that we ran, what we got back from line managers and learners themselves was that they loved the flexibility – they were able to fit the learning around shift patterns or around unforeseen demands. So for example, if you are delivering a classroom-based course and there is a sudden issue at a workplace, what tends to happen is that the member of staff is called back to the workplace – but when they were using the PSP in the workplace itself, all they needed to do was switch off the PSP, go and attend to the issue, come back and then recommence their learning. So they were able to fit the learning around the workplace. It meant that they didn't have to travel across the authority – they were actually doing their learning in their own workplace, and both managers and learners said that they really valued that. The most interesting thing was that the learners felt that they had far more control over their learning in terms of pace and place – they could choose.

"We got lots of comments from learners about liking the fact that they could go back and revisit materials as often as they wanted to, until they were clear that they had got the learning point – something that they also reported they would be less likely to do in a group.

"So lots and lots of positives about actually dealing with the logistics, but even more important for us, lots of positives about the learning – because the whole point about the project for us was to look at the comparison between learning in a central location in a classroom setting, then taking the learning back to the workplace – and actually learning in the environment in which you are going to apply it. And again, the learners said that they found it much easier to apply the learning when they were using the PSP, because they were actually doing the work in the place where they were going to apply the learning.

"So the whole premise of the project was 'Is this situated learning – does it have an impact?' And what we found was that it did very definitely have an impact.

"The system works by using the PSP as a media player, and the authoring system lets you associate what they call 'markers', which are glorified barcodes, with different types of media, and it uses the PSP camera to identify the marker and trigger the media.

"There are two main ways you can use the system – one is to enhance print-based materials – so you could take these barcodes and insert them into printed documents. The first time we saw it, it was being demonstrated with a tagged up version of a Shakespeare play, and you were able to point it at a marker and it would actually ... so if it was Act 1, Scene 1, you would see the

Royal Shakespeare Company actually acting out the scene before you read it yourself. That is one way you can use it.

"The other way is to put the barcodes on the physical environment itself and use the work environment as the trigger for learning. So for example, you could put one of the codes on a drugs cabinet, a locked drugs cabinet in a residential unit for older people – then when you point the camera at it, you can have a video of somebody talking to you, a member of staff, saying 'remember, when you take drugs out this cabinet you have got to fill in certain bits of paperwork – here is what that looks like – here is what you put in this part of the form or that part of form'. So what you are doing is actually delivering the learning as you are applying it.

"So the idea there is to get the distance between learning and application as short as possible."

The ease with which people could use the device made it even more appealing, he said.

"What we were really keen on was e-learning with no interface, so people didn't have to sit and get over their anxiety about using a keyboard or a mouse or a track pad. I mean basically if you have got an opposable thumb it can press the X button – that's you good to go, because literally all you need to do is point the camera at one of the markers and the media plays. And you can construct whole programmes of learning, which we actually did with the research project – we took one of Glasgow City's courses, the 'Violence and aggression and personal safety at work', and turned that into an annotated workbook which had the markers embedded in it, which allowed people to access rich media as they were learning."

The feedback from the project was very positive, he says.

"Managers loved the flexibility that the system offered – learners, managers ...and they liked the fact that they didn't have to send people across the authority to the training centre: it made the whole thing much, much more flexible for them. One manager even said that what they liked about it was there was no place to hide. What they meant was you couldn't turn up for a course and sit in the corner and coast all day; it was you, the learner and the learning, and you had to get on with it. The fact that somebody was learning was much more visible in the workplace, because they were using it in the workplace.

"And for learners, they really loved the sense of control and ownership, so they felt they were in control of their learning – they could dictate the pace, they could remediate if they wanted to, they didn't have to feel embarrassed about asking a question because there was no group sitting around – they could actually kind of ask the question of their line manager, so it got the line manager more involved, or they could talk to peers. In the demonstration project we had one workplace where there were two members of staff both using the system and they were able to bounce ideas off each other with that."

The low cost was also appealing…

"Well actually it's really cheap, which is what drew our attention to it. To buy a full kit, standard kit from Connected Education – a carry case, which also charges the devices, it includes 16 PSPs, cameras, memory sticks and the software, the authoring software to create the materials, the scripts – it's something like £3,500 to £4,000. And when we talked to training managers, they tell us that 'One course would pay for that – one day's training would pay for a whole kit'.

"And the other thing was that the authoring system and delivery system is a closed system, so it's very easy – there is virtually no learning curve to either author or user. So those were the main things that drew us to it."

Information gathering

Gathering information accounts for a large amount of informal learning. Employees will go 'hunting' for information, not because they want to learn it, but because they need it to accomplish a task. And, as hunters have done back to the dawn of history, they will hunt on territory that is familiar and has proved in the past to produce results. We tend to have a default pattern we use when we hunt for information. Many immediately go onto the internet, some ask a colleague, some look on the company intranet, and some go back to trusted books or manuals. If we fail to find what we want, we then go to our second source and so on until we give up, because the barriers between us and the information are higher than our motivation to find it.

This default pattern is one of the barriers that must be overcome when introducing new information sources to people. They must be given an initial positive experience of the new information source in order for it to be on their list of worthwhile sources for future use. Many people will need some kind of training or demonstration of a new resource so they can use it effectively, even if it is very simple to use. They need to see how it can fit into their workflow, and provide them with immediate benefit.

The internet has become a major source of information, and this trend is accelerating, particularly with the rise in use of mobile devices that can connect to the internet. The sheer volume and immediacy of the information changes the game considerably. One of the challenges is that not everyone knows how to search the internet effectively or quickly for reputable, relevant and usable information. Searching the internet effectively is a skill that needs to be learned, and many organizations are now realizing that information retrieval is worth including in formal learning programmes.

A key skill when gathering information, whether it is from the internet or elsewhere, is being able to recognize 'good' information amongst all the 'bad'. In earlier times, when making information generally available was a costly exercise, people took care with the quality of the information. This care meant that there was a much better chance of information being accurate. Now that the cost of publishing information, especially on the internet, is virtually nothing, a lot of information is published with little care or checks and balances, such as peer review.

The huge amount of information now available, and the fact that much of it has undergone little in the way of quality control, means that there is now a place for information aggregators. People with skills in a certain area can search for information that is 'good' and gather it together in one location. People looking for this specific kind of information can then save a huge amount of time by only looking at this curated or moderated content. And given how precious time is to people, these aggregation services are worth paying for. This accounts for the rise in subscription-based services, where credible information is pooled and then made available to paying users. The services are not really selling information; they are selling time.

Accessing individualized instruction

Individualized instruction encompasses any learning activity that helps people meet their own learner-specific outcomes without unneeded instruction and enables them to do so at their own pace. This could include print-, video-, or computer-based learning.

All that's needed is some way of matching individual learning needs with specific instructional material. One way to do this is to provide a learning content management system (LCMS) that serves up a library of reusable learning objects.

Kevin Oakes, author of *LCMS, LMS – They're not just acronyms but powerful systems for learning*[61] says a good LCMS should have the following qualities:

- Authoring and content-creation capabilities
- Support for a wide variety of content formats
- A robust model for creating and managing learning objects
- Scalable object repository (the database where everything gets stored)
- Good search-and-browse capabilities
- Ability to personalize delivery of content
- Detailed tracking and reporting capabilities.

Another way to provide individualized instruction is simply to leave it up to learners to identify their own needs and locate instructional materials they think will be useful.

Sound instructional material may come in the form of interactive tutorials, simulations, even drill-and-practice activities – anything that involves some kind of learner practice with system feedback.

Examples of instructional materials include:

- Video on DVD, VHS or via the internet
- Interactive tutorials on CD-ROM, DVD-ROM or the internet
- Print-based tutorials – particularly where learners are attempting to master computer software that makes it difficult to follow the tutorial and do hands-on exercises on a single screen at the same time.

Some organizations provide their own individualized instruction materials, while others either rely on external sources or let employees find their own. One can pick up a variety of skills on the internet for nothing or at low cost. Learners can also choose from among many software application training systems on the web.

Lunch gatherings

Lunchtime can be an informal learning opportunity. Employees at all levels often talk business as well as last night's television and sports results while they eat. Conversations about work can range from grumbling about annoyances to attempts to sort out workplace problems. Employees can also pick up useful information from people they may not otherwise have much chance to talk with.

Unless it's an organized affair, lunch is almost always very informal, and conversation will ebb and flow. Usually, there's no agenda or goal and the conversations tend to be driven by what's uppermost in people's minds and who they are lunching with. When people are relaxed and feel free to express themselves, they come across as authentic, and authenticity generates credibility. What people say during lunchtime conversations has great power.

Professional groups

Professional groups exist to provide professional development for their members through meetings with guest speakers, workshops and networking events. Members can learn informally through listening and discussing best practices, exploring new ideas, learning new skills and meeting like-minded individuals. Professional groups are often made up of people from different organizations and industries, so there is a fertile ground for benchmarking practices and learning about methods from other sectors.

Trial-and-error

Trial-and-error can sometimes be a very effective way to learn. Think of learning new software, for example. If you're already familiar with your company's operating system and software applications, you are often able to apply what you know to begin using the new program, and then pick up the differences by making and subsequently correcting mistakes. Since the learning is taking place in context, it often sticks.

However, trial-and-error can also be a very expensive way to learn: expensive in time, in the cost of mistakes and even the cost of reputation. And just because an error is made, there is no guarantee that the next trial will result in success.

Trial-and-error is such a fundamental part of the way we learn that it has been the source of many pithy sayings such as 'A person who never made a mistake never tried anything new' (Albert Einstein), and 'You must learn from the mistakes of others. You can't possibly live long enough to make them all yourself' (Samuel Levenson).

The key to effective trial and error learning is the feedback and reflection part of the cycle. It works well when this is built into the actual work process in some way.

Apprenticeship

The system of apprenticeship was first developed in the later Middle Ages and came to be supervized by craft guilds and town councils. A master craftsman was entitled to employ young people as an inexpensive form of labour in exchange for providing food, lodging and formal training in the craft. These days, most of the training is done while working for an employer, who helps the apprentices learn their trade or profession in exchange for their continuing labour for an agreed period after they have achieved measurable competencies.

But the concept of apprenticeship has also widened. For example, open source software is a highly effective platform for learning through apprenticeship, according to organizational change experts, John Hagel and John Seely Brown.[62] In their white paper, 'From push to pull – emerging models for mobilising resources', they explain how open-source programmers often start with code developed by others and then develop enhancements required for specific environments.

As the code is developed, it is posted for use by a broad community of more experienced programmers. In fact, programmers learn to write code in ways that facilitate reading by others – a key sensibility acquired in open-source efforts. Because the code can be executed right away, the developers receive rapid feedback.

Participants in open-source projects thus learn at four levels: they observe and work with the code of others; they observe their own code in action; they get feedback and commentary from others executing their code, and they have access to feedback and commentary from others regarding code developed by other open-source programmers. These participants begin as legitimate peripheral participants and, as they build their skills through creation of their own code, they advance to become coaches and mentors of others. In this manner, participants structure their own learning environments and they pull the resources required for learning when it is most relevant and useful for them.

Networking with suppliers

Suppliers are a great source of expert information that is often overlooked in the hunt for the best price for their products and services. And of course the information they have may be of use to other suppliers as well, which enhances the whole supply chain.

Toyota encourages its suppliers to share knowledge by creating information networks. The company has developed an infrastructure and variety of inter-organizational processes that facilitate the transfer of explicit and tacit knowledge within its supplier network.[63]

In recent years, Toyota has changed its knowledge creation strategy regarding its subsidiaries and affiliations around the globe – instead of merely transferring knowledge, it now taps into the tacit knowledge of local staff in its markets around the globe. Its new 'learn local, act global' strategy for international business development has proved successful for tapping rich local knowledge bases, thus ensuring its competitive edge and global lead in the car industry.[64]

Online help

Increasingly, employees go online for help with solving a problem or learning software application features. In the context of software, they might look at the software creator's website for help or online forums where other users have posted their solutions to the same problem.

The online help provided by software developers varies in type and quality. Many have an index of features or tasks and then point users to pages showing how to accomplish the task. Most will also provide screen shots and short videos. Some contain lessons, wizards or templates.

These can be built into the software application, installed as a separate database along with the application, or simply provided as a link to internet-based resources.

The help and solutions provided by members of the public are often confined to postings in which an individual describes the problem and asks members for solutions. Although the forum members might moderate the content, there's no way of checking whether or not the solutions work, other than comments from other forum users who have tried the solution.

Beyond computer software applications, online help might come in the form of Electronic Performance Support Systems (EPSS). An EPSS is one step beyond a normal context-sensitive help system. It includes more information about the current task in relation to what happens at that particular organization. It could include information about workflow or organization policies and procedures. It could be a wizard that walks users through a decision-making process, or specific information geared to a task, such as needs assessment, budget forecasting or generating reports and proposals.

Using wikis

The Central Intelligence Agency (CIA) launched a wiki, Intellipedia, in 2006 to enable its agents around the world to share knowledge, tips and ideas with each other.

Based on the same open-source software used to build Wikipedia, Intellipedia now hosts hundreds of thousands of pages and documents that can be accessed, read, edited and written by individuals with the appropriate security clearance.[65] The CIA is only one of the many US intelligence, diplomatic, and military organizations that use Intellipedia on 'top secret', 'secret' and 'unclassified' networks.

The Intellipedia effort was spearheaded by two CIA officers, Sean Dennehy and Don Burke, according to the CIA's official website. Its inspiration came from a 2004 award-winning paper by CIA employee Calvin Andrus entitled, 'The Wiki and the Blog: Toward a Complex Adaptive Intelligence Community'. The paper detailed the need for the intelligence community to adapt to the increased pace of the world.

There was a strong need within the intelligence community for more than analysis. "In addition to analysis, we need people who can create an ecosystem of knowledge that is not specifically about answering tomorrow's questions, but creating a world of information that is connected," Burke claimed.

Dennehy commented, "There's too much emphasis on the analytical report. It's important to look at how we get to the finished intelligence. Intellipedia does this by making the process more social and creating a dialogue that's transparent.

"It's not all about the wiki; it's about a suite of tools that has been made available to the US intelligence community," Dennehy said. "We looked at what works on the Internet and [said], 'Let's bring it in and see if it helps us do our jobs in informing policymakers."

Intellipedia had its problems. Earlier versions were considered hard to work with, and there was resistance from users who preferred older methods of communication and collaboration.[66] But it received raves for the way it provided up-to-date information and allowed agents to share intelligence and information across agency boundaries.

To encourage people to use Intellipedia, some CIA managers have offered incentives to internal users, according to Burke.[67] For example, one manager started a contest that provided creators of the best topical pages built on Intellipedia with a free dinner or other tokens. Contests were held for pages with the most edits and pages with the most views.

Many of the collaboration tools used by the intelligence community are based on open source code in an effort to minimize costs to the taxpayer, Dennehy told an annual international conference for the Wikimedia community in July 2012.[68] "I think we've done this on a shoestring budget over the past several years," he added.

Intellipedia has been credited with operational successes in the past few years. Thomas Fingar, Director of National Intelligence, cited the successful use of Intellipedia to develop an article on how Iraqi insurgents were using chlorine: "They developed it in a couple of days interacting in Intellipedia… no bureaucracy, no mother-may-I, no convening meetings. They did it and it came out pretty good. That's going to continue to grow."[69]

In a September 2007 testimony before the United States Congress, Michael McConnell, the Director of National Intelligence, cited the increasing use of Intellipedia among analysts and its ability to help experts pool their knowledge, from virtual teams, and make quick assessments.[70]

Diplopedia, also created in 2006, is a wiki run by the United States Department of State that includes more than 15,000 articles on foreign affairs subjects and 'diplomatic statecraft'.[71] According to the department's website, some 5,000 employees have contributed their knowledge and expertise to the wiki.

Last year, the department also launched Corridor, a closed social networking site that uses the open-source WordPress platform. It allows state employees to create profiles and share information with one another on a secure platform.

Westinghouse is another organization that has come to realize the benefit of knowledge sharing. It focuses heavily on building deep skills among nuclear power plant operators around the world.[72] The company understands that each of these individuals, while highly trained and certified, has tips and techniques developed over many years. Using BlackBoard, the company set up a simple knowledge-sharing portal to enable new plant operators to learn quickly from experts.

The Federal Reserve of Cleveland (part of the central banking system of the US) set up a similar system using Microsoft's SharePoint, but with added instructional content (for example, upfront tests and post-reading quizzes) around all user-driven content.

Communities of practice

Communities of practice are groups of people who come together to share and to learn from one another, face-to-face and virtually. They're held together by a common interest in a body of knowledge and are driven by a desire and need to share problems, experiences, insights, templates, tools and best practices. The members of such a community deepen their knowledge by interacting on an ongoing basis.[73]

These community networks are increasingly supported by collaboration tools, such as SharePoint sites, where knowledge, frequently asked questions and such like are captured in one source, edited and supported by the network itself.

The World Bank is an example of an organization that has used communities of practice within a strategic process of collaboration for learning. One of the main currencies of value within a community is the shared stories. What makes stories powerful is not just the knowledge within the story, but also the insights the story generates, especially when the story is discussed within the community. Knowledge is generated that would not have occurred without the community discussion.

The World Bank redefined its purpose to encompass establishing and maintaining a network of collaborative relationships motivated by knowledge sharing.

It had always offered development assistance in the form of a mix of finance and ideas to improve living standards. In 1996, its President announced that it would become the first point of contact for information and knowledge about development. This shift emphasized the importance of drawing on experience from other similar situations in the success of development projects.

The World Bank works within a network of other bodies also dedicated to development, including donor governments, non-governmental organizations, borrower governments and private sector groups. It set out to systematically capture and organize the knowledge and experience of staff, clients and development partners, with the aim of making this knowledge available and creating new collaborative links between network partners.

A basic infrastructure and set of programmes was established to share knowledge within the World Bank and with clients and partner organizations. These included:

- Communities of practice (both internal to the World Bank and with external individuals and groups)
- Advisory services to provide quick and easy access to resources
- Regional and country-level programmes to provide customized information and knowledge
- Initiatives to bring development practitioners from many organizations together, both face-to-face and virtually, to share experience and ideas.

These initiatives have been successful because they were aligned with the core business of the World Bank and because collaboration clearly added value to each member of the network.[74]

Steve Denning, the bank's former director of knowledge management, observes that "internal knowledge sharing improves our efficiency, but sharing it externally has a much larger impact, improving our quality of service and reaching a much wider group of clients."[75]

Improving information sharing through social networking

Dixons Retail in the UK is a fast-moving, market-leading retailer, specializing in electrical goods and computing. The organization works with over 10,000 different products, with new ones constantly being added as the latest technology develops. Building and retaining a knowledge base for their staff is a key strand of their strategy to continually improve the customer experience.

Dixons had been focusing on e-enabling the organization's formal training strategy, initially for the organization's 16,000 retail staff, who operate from 700 outlets. This has since been extended to thousands more staff working in head office, contact centres, home service and distribution. It was clear that the organization had to embrace more online learning, so a formal learning strategy was developed, focusing on the way that employees actually learn in their day-to-day jobs.[76]

Boyd Glover, Head of Learning at Dixons Retail, comments that "Prior to introducing learning technologies, the organization relied heavily on a catalogue of classroom courses, but these were costly and time consuming, and the pick-and-mix approach to training didn't meet the ongoing needs of colleagues or indeed customers. What we needed was a learning offering that didn't just deliver more for less, but could also be more aligned to support individuals on the job."

He adds, "We knew our colleagues were happy to share and were already doing so via Facebook and other social networks; the challenge for us was what were they sharing? Colleagues passing the wrong information to each other could easily damage the customer experience. The challenge for Dixons became how do we harness the love of sharing but ensure that the right information is being shared? The organization has its fair share of experts but how do you get them to share the knowledge that they have?"

Another challenge was choosing the right platform. The top search engine in use is Google, followed by YouTube, but these sites are in the public domain, creating concerns about public access to internal information. It was clear that Dixons had to replicate the opportunities that external sites offer for sharing and rating, but they were looking for an environment that created a protected and private corporate YouTube (with aspects of LinkedIn) for Dixons employees.

Dixons decided to trial the Fuse platform, a video-centric social platform that builds on the concepts of popular social networking sites. The platform enables video content to be created, shared and rated, and has the potential to support an informal learning strategy in a number of different ways – providing support for colleagues in the work place when they are looking to apply learning, addressing concerns when things go wrong and helping them to adapt quickly when things have changed.

In terms of informal learning in the stores, there is plenty of anecdotal evidence of success. The video-editing creativity of colleagues has shone through and the team has responded well to being trusted to contribute. One store member commented "I can't believe you let me do this – thank you!!" Colleagues have also exhibited great responsibility as a result of having their videos published. Those who have contributed video ideas that have been rated well, have worked hard to live up to the expectations of their colleagues by continuing to share ideas and illustrate their own ongoing successes. Those who contributed videos that were not rated as well have often raised their game and resubmitted them.

And the results? The stores that participated in the early pilots increased the average laptop sale price by 30 per cent compared with those who did not. In other words, customers spent more per transaction buying a higher specification machine and extra accessories.

For Dixons, it is not a question of informal or formal learning; it is both. The integration of the two is an ongoing process, driven by innovative thinking, powered by technology and focused on supporting and building performance.

Steve Dineen, The CEO of Fusion Universal who supply the Fuse platform said "It was an amazing opportunity to work with Dixons and push the boundaries of social and workplace learning."

The following tips are copied from the Dixons case study prepared by Towards Maturity, an independent, not-for-profit organization, with the goal of helping others to improve the impact of learning technologies at work.

1. Introduce new innovations by aligning the outputs with strategic business initiatives.
2. Create a culture for learning – build on previous successes with formal online learning.
3. Encourage a seamless fit with formal learning programmes.
4. Pump prime the system by creating a framework to incentivize contributions – set a challenge or create a competition.
5. Trust your staff to rise to the challenge to encourage others.
6. Allow trust to build – look for evidence of individual and business success and share it all the time.
7. Provide opportunities for learning and development staff to experience the benefits in their own work environment to help overcome resistance.
8. Consider restructuring L&D roles to help facilitate the sharing of effective practices.
9. Work with IT to identify appropriate solutions and to trial video on existing platforms.
10. Don't be afraid of working in the cloud to help overcome IT infrastructure challenges.
11. Don't limit your expectations of how staff will access the programme – ensure it is accessible 24/7 and via all main devices.
12. Spend time with HR, business partners, directors and other stakeholders to keep the profile of the programme high.
13. Continually work with stakeholders to improve and identify new ways of harnessing the opportunities for informal learning in the business.

In another example, the United States Office of the Director of National Intelligence (ODNI) introduced iVideo, a YouTube-like application, to improve how information is shared throughout the intelligence agency.[77] It joins a host of online collaboration tools that the ODNI has released in recent years. These include a photo-sharing application similar to Flickr, a tool for bookmarking web pages that is similar to del.icio.us, instant messaging, blogging software, and Intellipedia, the Wikipedia of the intelligence community.

Don Burke, one of the two CIA officers who spearheaded the launch of Intellipedia, also helped lead testing and implementation of iVideo at the CIA. He said, "Just like on the real Web, if you want to upload photos, you tend to go to Flickr. If you want to upload videos, you go to YouTube. If you want to get an encyclopaedic entry, you go to Wikipedia. It's the same thing on the intelligence community networks now."

Officials said they had high hopes for iVideo which, like Intellipedia, is available on three networks: 'top secret', which is used by members of the 16 federal intelligence agencies who have the appropriate clearance; 'secret', used by many employees of the Defense and State departments, and 'sensitive but unclassified', which is open to government employees generally and to invited guests.

Sean Dennehy, the CIA's Intellipedia and Enterprise 2.0 evangelist who, along with Burke, is leading the agency's effort to incorporate the new tools, said, "It's been pretty remarkable how people have gravitated to it, and it shows that there actually was a need for this capability.

"This is kind of grass-roots adoption. One of the things that we encourage with all of these tools is for people to find value in the tools themselves rather than it being forced upon them from up on high."

According to Burke, iVideo brings an important improvement to the intelligence community by standardizing the way video is shared using Adobe's Flash. There is no comparable government-wide standard.

"If someone in Tokyo has video that needs to get back to headquarters, they can upload it to this site and then it would be not only accessible to headquarters, but accessible to the entire network and then people could, using the comments, be able to start a discussion about that video and what the implications of that video are," says Dennehy.

He and Burke say video also allows for better communication and keeps the intelligence community from being overly reliant on text documents.

"We as a community don't want to be solely based on text," says Dennehy. "We also want to incorporate visual graphics and other instances, and video is just another extension for that."

They would like eventually to move the intelligence agencies' massive amounts of video to the networks. However, users have so far mainly shared training videos, sent messages regarding employee conduct and done some intelligence sharing.

"It's too early to tell exactly how it'll be used, but there are already instances where people have shared direct intel-related videos," says Burke. "So I would suspect that would be a very big use of it."

The virtual classroom

Providing employees with access to an open learning exchange is how one network service and solutions provider known to the author found a way to get around its training budget constraints. The learning exchange was created with a few goals in mind – giving leaders an alternative to formalized learning, taking advantage of expertise within the community, and harvesting knowledge within the community.

The learning platform now offers over 5,000 pieces of informal learning, most of which are aimed at increasing productivity, aiding sales and technical support, and providing internal marketing. Any employee can contribute to the site, and the formats of learning bites include PDFs, podcasts and video. The media is also downloadable via iTunes, thereby creating a mobile platform.

Senior executives use the site to publish brief weekly videos in which they communicate directions and strategies to employees. This is particularly useful to the workforce, half of which works from home.

The company's formal course curriculum leverages its informal content. Course delegates get access to a portal which is a compendium of informal information, including links to books and news, tag clouds and media, much of which has been launched formally by being broken down into course-like structures. By doing that, the company's learning team slashed its programme development time by 90 per cent.

Knowledge sharing

Canon uses its daily morning meeting (Asakai) of senior managers as a way to encourage the sharing of tacit knowledge.

Ikujiro Nonaka, Professor Emeritus, Hitotsubashi University Graduate School of International Corporate Strategy[78] told delegates at the International Productivity Conference (2007) that at those meetings there is no set agenda. Instead, executives are encouraged to bring up whatever is on their minds or express opposite points of view – ideals and the reality, constraints and possibilities, internal capability and market opportunities.

"These are debated from many perspectives and combined," he said. "If some issues are not solved at Asakai, they are quickly transferred to a variety of formal meetings, such as management strategy meetings.

"Consequently, Asakai meetings are linked to a variety of meetings within Canon in a multi-layered way, making it (the meeting content) open, expanding and extending it to larger groups and spreading knowledge quickly, like a 'small-world network'.

"Small-world network theory means any two people can be connected through common links of friendship. It is a very fast way to spread not only explicit knowledge but tacit knowledge as well."

He went on to explain that during lunchtimes Fujio Mitarai, CEO of Canon, holds management strategy meetings that include division and section heads.

"It has almost 100 per cent attendance because everybody has to eat lunch anyway. Most of the time the attendees eat Japanese udon noodles – or very simple foods like sushi. They eat in five minutes and then have 55 minutes to talk. All the leaders are linked: that is their way."

Documentation

Documentation refers to the policies, processes, procedures, product descriptions, product plans, reports and similar materials describing the operations of an organization and the products and services that organization offers. These sources are often a primary tool that workers use to informally learn about their jobs.

One medium-sized electronics firm created their ISO documentation with maximum employee input: each employee was asked to write down the procedure that he or she followed, and the document then went through a series of edits between management and worker.

The final document provided useful, job-specific information, with an emphasis on local (rather than general) skills information, because it was initiated by the person actually performing the particular set of skills.

Employees stated that during on the job cross-training, they referred to these documents as often as they asked their trainer because they knew that someone who actually worked on the machine had written the document.

Job execution

At a mid-sized manufacturing site, employees who were required to perform routine, repetitive tasks on a production line were motivated in the daily execution of their jobs and encouraged to think proactively, critically and analytically. This was emphasized by their work team leader and supervisor, as well as the supporting engineer and skilled workers.

Through the supervisor and work team leader, the company goal – to exceed the expected productivity rate – and certain policies, such as cooperation and teamwork, were clearly and consistently communicated to the employees. The supporting line engineer also encouraged employees to work with him to come up with improved ways to do their jobs. And skilled workers explained certain basic mechanical and electrical elements of the machinery to enable workers to repair minor breakages.

As a result, each employee on the line actively sought out new, refined and streamlined ways to work at their task and meet the company goals. The daily execution of their task, no matter how repetitive, became an exercise in identifying, analysing, thinking and implementing new ideas.

Job shadowing

At the technology research firm Forrester, novice researchers pair up with experienced researchers, and everyone works in a completely open, transparent physical work environment, with no office or cubicle walls to hinder the shadowing and learning process.[79]

Job shadowing is a powerful method of passing wide-ranging complex skills, knowledge and attitudes from experts to novices, giving the new people an opportunity to watch the more experienced ones for extended periods.

It may seem inappropriate to saddle your best experts with shadow duty, because there will be an inevitable impact on their productivity, but it does ensure that new starters will pick up essential core skills and attitudes right from the beginning. This will also help foster cultural continuity, which is an often overlooked aspect of the benefits of job shadowing.

Employees can also job observe – watching an expert do the job. Shadowing, by comparison, involves a little more interactivity, whereby the shadow is given the opportunity to try the task or at least query the expert. This is similar in approach to the long-established apprenticeship approach to learning.

The help desk

The help desk is probably the most institutionalized mode of informal learning for software applications. Ideally, it should provide the one-on-one helping hand or bit of advice that many ordinary users need from time to time.

Help desks can be internal, organized as part of the information technology or other department, or external, provided by software or hardware vendors. Internal help desks can provide more targeted support and often respond more quickly and personally than external organizations. They are also prevalent as part of customer service organizations, for all kinds of product support, from furniture to appliances – anything that requires some technical skill to assemble or operate.

When it comes to employee performance support, help desks tend to be relegated to technology. But there's no reason why other arenas can't benefit from organized performance support as well; they can equally well be used to provide informal, individualized support for other tasks people need to do only infrequently, including soft skills.

In larger organizations, help desks can also provide follow-up support for training programmes. For example, an employee might have attended a workshop, but back in the office might be unsure how to apply what he or she learned. The help desk can suggest tools and identify the relevant issues.

A more wide-ranging form of help desk is the Employee Assistance Programme (EAP), where employees are able to call an external provider with any query at all, from health and wellbeing issues through to moving house issues. This can be a first port of call for employees to ask about how to handle incidents involving bullying or harassment and issues can also include health, marital, family, financial, alcohol, drug, legal, emotional, stress or other personal matters.

The EAP Association website says that the support services offered by an EAP will generally consist of a blend of the following:

- Short-term psychological services, such as counselling
- Money advice and debt management
- Child and elderly care information services
- Legal information and guidance
- Information on emotional, work-life and workplace issues
- Assessment, support, short-term counselling and referral for employee issues
- Management referrals and support
- Case management of all ongoing cases, to ensure the assessment, treatment and support requirements are carried out to EAPA quality standards
- Utilization reporting
- Management information on employee and organizational interventions, including consultation with management on behavioural aspects of the workplace
- Working to the confidentiality and ethical standards promoted by EAPA.

Over the years, EAPs have become an integral tool in many organizations' attempts to engage employees and support the health and wellbeing of their workforce. In fact, the latest independent research commissioned by EAPA UK (2008) reveals that 5,200 organizations – representing over 8.2 million employees – now enjoy the services of an EAP.

Informal coaching

Informal coaching helped a computer company cut employee turnover in half and significantly boost sales revenue per employee. Before the introduction of the informal coaching programme, the company found that its sales organization was suffering high turnover, low revenue attainment and low morale.[80]

The company was considering a new sales training programme. Its Chief Learning Officer studied the problem and realized that the problem was not one of core skills (many of its sales professionals were quite senior), but rather one of managerial skills, coaching and culture. Extensive interviews revealed that sales management at the company was not a highly-regarded role and expert sales professionals were promoted without adequate training.

He created a highly-interactive simulation-based coaching programme that taught all sales managers how to coach, develop, diagnose and support their sales teams. The programme used a combination of self-study, team projects and expert-led coaching (with very little formal training). During a nine-month programme period, each team was empowered to work on local projects, after which they came together and compared their results.

Each team had a series of challenges to address, and both managers and salespeople collaborated on solutions.

Informal coaching does not take place in scheduled appointments, but in everyday workplace conversations. These conversations may be short or long, one-to-one or within a group, task-focused or people-focused. What qualifies them as coaching is not a formal model or structure, but a style of conversation, according to business coach Mark McGuiness.[81]

He makes the point that "When the approach is used implicitly, as part of the everyday conversation between the manager and her team, it may be that neither party would describe the conversation as 'coaching'." By comparison, the most obvious characteristic of formal business coaching is that it is being used explicitly. In other words, during the session, both parties are clear that they are engaged in 'coaching' and are committed to this process as well as the outcome. Formal coaching, therefore, usually takes place during scheduled appointments.

McGuiness adds that although some people might be uncomfortable with the word 'coaching' or with the idea of being coached, they usually respond well to a manager who takes the time to listen carefully to them, asking questions that empower them to find their own way of meeting a challenge or solving a problem without being told what to do. "Or a manager might be so familiar with this approach or it might be so similar to her natural communication style that she may not consciously decide to 'coach' someone but instinctively listen and ask rather than 'tell and sell'."

Supervision style

The way in which people are supervised has a big impact on what they learn. The phrase Management by Wandering Around (MBWA) was coined for the activity of randomly visiting employees at their work stations and answering and asking questions.

Through these interactions, employees learn about various company policies and solutions to workplace problems or technical questions. Receiving instant on-the-job feedback and instruction from an expert means employees feel positive about implementing ideas and are reassured to know that a proficient manager is their immediate supervisor.

Alongside this, an open-door policy on the part of the supervisor encourages communication and information exchange. An accessible supervisor will make it much easier for employees to learn what they need to know in terms of job basics and company policies.

Cross-training and job swaps

An example of cross-training would be a factory floor where all employees are encouraged to perform the work at every machine in their work unit. Employees learn the operating procedures of various machines and thus new segments of the production process (which gives them an overview of the whole production process). Cross-training can also create a sense of team-work among employees as they help each other at the different work stations and develop productive social and interaction skills, as well as interpersonal dynamics.

There is an obvious advantage to the company in having their employees skilled at many different jobs, and employees often like the opportunity to move around and do different jobs, especially when these are repetitive and potentially boring.

A useful addition can be to implement a recognition scheme, with badges, job titles and pay rises for those employees who master several different jobs.

Cross-functional and cross-divisional movement

At Nike, cross-functional and cross-divisional movement is seen as especially valuable.[82] Line managers periodically get together to discuss where their people might best fit in new stretch opportunities in other parts of the organization or under the supervision of other managers.

Although the process started out to target only leadership candidates, many divisions of the company have now adopted it to support all employees.

Social learning

Increasingly, IBM is leveraging social learning to contribute to their learning strategy. Rather than develop centrally-related content, experts throughout the company find, build, publish, share and comment on assets, to enhance skills development and productivity.

IBM has created tools, such as online learning communities and socially-generated tags on key knowledge assets, to make relevant knowledge more searchable. It has also reduced search time and costs, accelerated on-boarding and, recognizing that more than 40 per cent of its workforce is global, enabled delivery of job-relevant information to networked mobile devices.

The Cheesecake Factory, a US restaurant group, uses something it calls the 'Video Café' to encourage its employees to share information via social media.[83] Michael Rose, former GM of social learning platform Knoodle, explains that the Video Café is an informal learning portal that allows employees to film, upload and watch short videos generated by their peers on a variety of different job-related topics, from how to greet customers to how to slice and serve cheesecakes. Not only does this method reduce the cost and time it takes to develop original content, it encourages a continuous learning culture in which employees can continue to learn tips and best practice from peers – all through small multimedia snippets of information.

Formalized coaching

An IT management and solutions company had a poorly-managed sales environment. Within the sales staff, revenue was low, attrition was high and there were low levels of employee satisfaction.

After some investigation, the problems were identified as communication- rather than skills-related. It was decided to create a formalized coaching programme in which managers were forced to coach sales representatives on a weekly basis.

The results showed dramatic improvement. There was a huge uptake in employee engagement; turnover went down, and revenue went up. Very little formal training was involved – the majority of it was informal, but harnessed within a formal structure.

In another example, Coventry Building Society designated five of the 50 employees in its call centre as full-time manager-coaches.[84] In this new role, they provide two hours of coaching each week to every employee by listening to calls and providing immediate feedback and suggestions for improvement. Although the number of people taking calls went down, the call centre's performance went up.

Peer coaching

Peer coaching involves individuals with similar status giving each other feedback and advice. This may alleviate some of the anxiety involved when coaching has the potential to get mixed up with performance evaluations, such as in the situation where a superior acts as the coach or mentor.

Input from peers is valuable because they will often notice things about us that we do not see in ourselves. This makes peer coaching of particular value when it is being used to foster relationship and communication skills.

It can be a spur-of-the-moment thing, or it could be on a more explicit level, where two employees have agreed to give each other feedback when it seems appropriate.

Asking colleagues in the office for help

Unlike peer coaching, asking a colleague for help is as simple and unstructured as walking over to their desk or popping into their office with a quick question.

The interaction is usually brief, but may occur frequently and develop into (or result from) an ongoing relationship between colleagues. Besides skills and knowledge, these interactions help foster community and collaboration.

Mentoring

While mentoring is not a new concept, McDonald's has taken it into the 21st century by introducing and offering a web-based tool used for matching, tracking, and facilitating advisor/learner (mentor/mentee) relationships across the entire organization.[85]

Its programme incorporates the latest technology features of both informal and formal mentoring approaches, providing a virtual environment to encourage career engagements (one-to-one), topical engagements (group/peer learning/sharing), and situational engagements (short-term, special projects) that benefit individuals, groups and, of course, McDonald's.

At Microsoft, many employees have mentors. HR facilitates the mentoring process by giving employees a web-based matching tool that provides them with potential mentors (using blinded profiles) every five to six months. The practice is optional and driven and performed by employees themselves. Coaching is also no longer reserved just for executives.[86]

Flash mentoring

Flash mentoring is defined as a one-time meeting or discussion that enables an individual to learn and seek guidance from a more experienced person, who can pass on relevant knowledge and experience.[87]

The purpose of flash mentoring is to provide a valuable learning opportunity for less experienced individuals, while requiring a limited commitment of time and resources for more experienced individuals serving as mentors.

While mentors and mentees can mutually decide to meet again after their flash mentoring session, the only commitment is to participate in the initial meeting. The term 'flash mentoring' was coined by K Scott Derrick, Director of Professional Development at the Senior Executives Association (SEA) in Washington, DC, in his work with 13L, a group of mid-career US federal employees, passionate about leadership and leadership development.

The standard flash mentoring session involves a one-time meeting or discussion – in person or using telecommunications technologies – between a more experienced individual (the mentor) and a less experienced individual (the mentee).

A flash mentoring session can last from a few minutes to a couple of hours. The pairing of the mentor and mentee is usually arranged informally, without any commitment on the part of the mentor or mentee to stay in contact or meet again, although they sometimes do so as an outgrowth of their discussion. There are numerous variations of flash mentoring approaches.

In sequential flash mentoring, the mentee is paired with more than one mentor for a series of one-time meetings or discussions with each. For example, a mentee could participate in one-time flash mentoring sessions with four different mentors, once per month over a four-month period. A variation of sequential flash mentoring is speed mentoring, where mentors and mentees meet for only a few minutes and then rotate to another mentor/mentee immediately afterwards, and so on.

In group flash mentoring, a mentor is paired with a small group of mentees for a one-time meeting or discussion. A variation of this flash mentoring technique is group speed mentoring, where a mentor meets with a small group of mentees for, say, 20 minutes and then rotates to another group of mentees immediately afterwards and so on.

In autumn 2008, the Senior Executives Association (SEA) launched a new flash mentoring programme for its members. Under the programme, active and retired SEA members volunteered approximately one hour of their time to meet one-on-one (in person or via telephone) with newly-appointed members of SEA who were seeking advice on personal growth and career development. Both mentor and mentee committed to only a one-time meeting, but they could mutually agree to stay in touch if they chose. SEA followed up with all mentors and mentees to ask them about their experiences with the flash mentoring session. The feedback that came from almost all of the participants was overwhelmingly positive.

Heterogeneous teams

Teaming newbies with more experienced colleagues can be very effective at fostering learning, but it's not easy on either the beginners or the experts. Often, what tends to happen is that the experts are trying to get on with the job quickly and efficiently, while the novices are slowing things down even though they are trying to keep up.

It works if everyone knows that the purpose of creating heterogeneous teams is to foster learning. It is essential that the experienced employees understand that they get benefits from participating, including the recognition of their expert status, and also the opportunity to learn while teaching. It is an old adage that the best way to learn something is to teach it. It is often surprising to old hands what they can learn from someone who comes at the skill from a fresh perspective, asking questions that challenge existing assumptions.

The team roles can be designed to evolve over time, as with apprenticeships of old, where the apprentice began doing menial tasks while watching the expert as much as possible. As the modern day apprentice grows more skilled, he or she takes on increasing responsibility.

Case studies

The case study method can be implemented top-down within an organization to capture institutional knowledge. It works by using direct, timely examples to help an employee improve a skill or work at a problem. Meetings with a supervisor occur on a monthly or weekly one-on-one basis, providing time to discuss what worked, what didn't, and what changes could be made as a result. The tenets of the method are follow-up and use of ad hoc case studies, rather than rehashed, dated examples.

This system can be implemented at any level or in any function within an organization.

Action learning groups

Small groups (five or six people) form across different functions, but within similar levels of an organization. Their purpose is to help facilitate the transfer of new ideas into an applied setting in the workplace. The groups meet for half-day sessions and discuss real issues and their solutions. In effect, it is a form of peer coaching within a facilitated structure.

It gives people the opportunity to reflect and crystallize learning in the workplace and put things into practice. Employees have the chance to incorporate new knowledge in the presence of those with similar experiences. They can share and revise best practices in the company of their peers.

The return-on-investment of such groups can be measured through a high-performance environment scan, before and after the method is first used.

Other types of measurement are coaching or leadership 360-degree feedback mechanisms, as well as seeking both qualitative and quantitative feedback from delegates in the programmes.

Informal feedback

At Hewlett-Packard and Intel, individuals are encouraged to actively seek feedback from those they work with and then to synthesize and reflect on the feedback without it being routed through HR. As the practice is driven and maintained by each individual employee, performance management is completely customized, as well as integrated with the business.

Incidental meetings between departments

At Pixar, Steve Jobs oversaw the design of the new building. Because the software people worked in one area and the marketing people worked in another, he decided to put the toilets in a central atrium. That way, employees had to run into each other each day and presumably chat.

When workspaces aren't designed to facilitate incidental meetings between colleagues, information doesn't flow. Jay Cross gives the example of a high tech company that realized employees just weren't talking.[88]

"I pointed out that their meeting rooms were always booked solid, everyone worked out of small cubicles, and there simply wasn't a decent place for conversations to take place. I suggested they rip out a quarter of the cubicles and replace them with leather sofas, portable white boards, and espresso machines. I'm convinced it would have helped them prosper, but I'll never know. They didn't invite me back."

Conversations

Conversations can play a strong role in performance and productivity.

The role of conversation as a power tool for improvement is often overlooked in performance solution design. Its power can be exploited everywhere, from coffee-break conversations and informal mentoring by colleagues and managers to structured exchanges and expert knowledge-sharing sessions.

The effective use of conversations is part of one of the most important challenges L&D teams face in producing effective solutions to business problems. To move from focusing on knowledge acquisition towards facilitating the development of 'real' learning and understanding, any solution needs to fully engage workers in the development process. This includes providing opportunities for them to think about the different outcomes that could have resulted from a set of circumstances. Conversations are a great way to facilitate this process.

Pfizer's 1,200 managers have learned to have more effective conversations, according to Cross.[89] The managers took part in an instructor-led programme called 'Courageous Conversations'. Although the programme involved workshops that lasted from two hours to a full day, reinforcement and the real lessons were learned informally, after the workshop.

Pfizer believes it is essential for line leaders to have "the robust ability to engage in highly skilful conversations around challenging issues".

"Conversation is the most powerful instructional technology on the planet," Cross says. "Business people learn better and deeper when they converse with the right people. Yet most firms don't have a directory of who knows what to make it easy for people to find the right people to talk to.

"This is Knowledge Management 101, for heaven's sake. Who do most knowledge workers turn to when they need an answer to a question? Whoever is physically closest to them. What are the odds that your neighbour has the answer? That's why most questions go unanswered or, worse, receive the wrong answer. This is not ethereal; it's common sense."

Content provision

Another way to provide employees with just-in-time learning resources is via informal 'learning bites' in the form of articles, videos and podcasts. These give them the opportunity to learn skills and strategies on a wide range of issues and topics.

The learning bites might be either purchased via subscription from an outside supplier or developed in house. Whatever the source, the real key to success lies in making them easy to access when and where people will find them most useful. This is typically close, in time and place, to where the information will be used, so the content becomes a just-in-time support resource.

And the content provided need not be only bite-sized. If it is structured well, the navigation and ease of search of the content will enable a user to get the immediate piece of information they need, and then perhaps go back later, when they have more time and/or more experience in using the information, to seek a deeper and broader understanding.

Private social network

The ACCA (Association of Chartered Certified Accountants), a global body for professional accountants, adopted the private social network Yammer to connect its 1,000 employees and encourage them to communicate.

Interestingly, the move to Yammer came about, not from the company's L&D department nor its internal communications team, but from an employee in one of its UK offices.

"From there it went viral with early adopters choosing to use it as they saw the value for themselves and the reputation spread," according to Rachel Millar, an internal communications professional, writing in her 'Diary of an internal communicator' blog.[90]

The ACCA's Internal Communications Manager, Suzanne Masters, comments: "Within ACCA, we have matrix management; we work on different projects and cross-functional teamwork is fantastic but presents its challenges. We had a number of ways of getting feedback from employees, one of which was a question in our employee survey on whether best practice, good ideas and ways of doing things were shared across the company. The results showed we could do better and we introduced Yammer as part of the solution to this problem."

Three employee needs were identified: they needed somewhere to go to find out who colleagues were and what they looked like, they wanted a platform to share information while avoiding duplication and starting from scratch, and they wanted to be able to identify expertise, with a central base for shared information.

Although the company had an intranet, held virtual events and face-to-face sessions, and published an e-zine, none of these specifically tackled the needs they'd identified. It was using LinkedIn to connect its 140,000 members, but wasn't using it internally.

Masters said: "We did a quick survey on Yammer and asked 'how is this for you' to gather feedback and ideas from employees. This was a low key start and the survey meant we were able to see if there was anything we needed to take into consideration before launching 'officially' internally."

She developed a business case in order to have the paid-for version of Yammer, which includes an appointed administrator, working with ACCA's IT team, legal team and HR. Masters says the key point for her was that they are a global organization and wanted to work together more, but they didn't have a tool that allowed this to happen.

The scheme was given the go-ahead, with the proviso it could only be used for work purposes. An email from ACCA's Strategy Director was sent to encourage employees to use it and to let them know it was 'allowed', though participation wasn't mandatory. It also had to be integrated into comms plans and never used as the sole means of communication, but alongside other existing channels.

Certain governance issues have to be constantly addressed, for example removing an employee's email address if they leave the company, and ensuring that only permanent staff, not contractors, are able to access Yammer, due to concerns over confidential information.

Employee business networks

McDonald's has a long history of supporting and building its employee business networks.[91] These networks began as and continue to be voluntary, interrelated groups of employees, who provide support and act as advocates for the employees they represent. In addition, they serve to provide a sense of community within McDonald's among the participants. Additionally, they now provide information, education and advice for both the employees and the company.

They have also aligned themselves with the company's strategic business plans and have positioned themselves as networks that can positively impact the bottom line of McDonald's.

Chapter 5

The new L&D role

"We are not in the business of providing classes, learning tools, or even learning itself. We are in the business of facilitating improved business results."

Fred Harburg

Essentially, Learning & Development should be an enabler of business performance, influencing and responding to the organization's capability agenda. In reality, unfortunately, L&D is all too often preoccupied with programmes and products, rather than supporting the needs of the organization.

L&D professionals need to assume responsibility for making a difference in the organization. Successful L&D people recognize the opportunity to add value and develop strategies to demonstrate value in the organization. Unsuccessful L&D personnel struggle to align what they do with the organization, offering programmes that are not connected with the realities of the workplace. The result is that learning is dispersed, disorganized and disconnected, and fails to add value to the bottom line. The learning that does take place within L&D initiatives often does not transfer well back into the workplace.

L&D personnel now need to move from being providers of training to being strategic partners in the organization. Their mandate has to be to improve the organization's performance by assisting people to become more capable, which is not necessarily the same as assisting people to become more knowledgeable. To accomplish this complex role, they need a combination of learning and business competencies.

The amount of available information is changing the world and with it the way L&D needs to operate. Traditional approaches to learning are slow and unresponsive, making people wait for the information they need, rather than giving it to them at their moment of need. L&D must support the people in organizations so that in turn they are supporting the organization in being agile and responsive to change.

Success comes from people being capable in the moment when faced with a task. The employee needs to bring the exact capability to bear on the presenting task right there and then. The new role of L&D is to ensure that this 'capability in the moment' happens.

The majority of learning that takes place in an organization is going on outside any formal L&D interventions anyway, so L&D needs to spread its influence into the learning that is happening informally, and thereby assist people be capable when and where they need to be.

This means that L&D needs to take charge of the learnscape and create a culture of capability. Capability is far more than just learning, although both formal and informal learning play significant parts. For example, the culture within which an employee operates has a bearing on their capability, and the key to culture at the employee level is their immediate manager. If the manager's behaviour has an impact on individual capability, then I would suggest that influencing management behaviour to enhance capability is part of the new L&D role.

Essentially the new L&D role is all about enablement: enabling workers, managers and the senior team. It may even extend to enabling suppliers and customers.

To meet those challenges, L&D professionals need a range of skills:

- Stakeholder management
- Performance consulting
- Creative thinking

- Collaboration
- Information management
- Problem-solving
- New media literacy.

Ultimately, the goal is improved performance, achieved through real-time capability.

What CEOs want

CEOs regard the way knowledge is managed within an organization to be of critical importance to its success. A study by John E. Lindholm, William G. Wallick and William J. Rothwell of CEOs' perceptions of their individual organization's major business challenges revealed they believed the following six were most pressing:[92]

1. Customer satisfaction.
2. Technology.
3. Globalization .
4. Profits/cost reduction.
5. Knowledge management.
6. Attracting, retaining and improving the performance of employees.

How L&D can contribute to meeting business challenges

In *What CEOs Expect from Corporate Training*, Rothwell and his co-authors suggest L&D professionals need to do the following:

- Understand the products and services of the organization
- Understand the company's business issues
- Facilitate business model changes
- Understand the company's culture
- Increase workplace learning to attract new people to the organization
- Regularly consult with customers
- Keep customers in the forefront of planned learning
- Evaluate technological trends and use what they learn to help change the business

- Communicate the technological trends to the organization
- Manage company-wide transition
- Create a continual learning environment
- Provide mentoring and coaching.

CEOs expect L&D to have a working knowledge of the organization's products or services and of the financial issues it faces. They also believe that the amount and quality of workplace learning helps in the attraction and retention of employees.

L&D needs to find ways to facilitate the sharing of knowledge, providing skills training, developing the thinking and creative processes of organizational members, using technology effectively and assisting the organization to find and retain high-performing employees.

In addition, CEOs believe L&D professionals should consult regularly with customers and other people who are recipients of the products and services that the organization provides to make sure that their needs and requests are at the forefront of learning initiatives.

Core competencies for L&D

Rothwell and his research team identified seven competencies from the CEO interviews as the most salient for increasing organizational performance through learning interventions.

1. Business knowledge

These abilities are reflected in the identification and organization of workforce capabilities and in the assessment of the workforce's strengths and weaknesses for meeting organizational goals.

L&D professionals need to analyse the current business environment, understand the organization's work processes and the performance gaps within those processes, and then plan for the future training and learning needs of the organization.

They also need to understand the organization's business operations and how it makes money or, in the case of public sector organizations, how they best serve their 'customers'.

They need to demonstrate this competency by aligning performance improvement interventions with the organization's strategy, business goals and work processes. Essentially, CEOs want L&D professionals to link learning efforts directly with the organization's goals.

2. Interpersonal/leadership

This competency enables individuals to interact effectively with other individuals and groups. When people have strong interpersonal abilities and business competency, they can be involved (as equals) in senior-level decision-making processes. L&D professionals need to interact with managers, line managers, supervisors and others to build interest in the organization's learning programmes and to uncover opportunities to collect information on learning needs.

3. Broad perspective

L&D professionals need to be able to assimilate many experiences into learning approaches, and to be open-minded, viewing employees as assets and having an awareness of the organization's culture. They need to understand the needs of customers and then be able to find out where deficiencies lie within the organization, so they can determine how best to assist learning to overcome those deficiencies. The learning environment they create must be easily accessed by employees.

4. Assessment

L&D professionals need to measure, assess and guide both individual and organizational workforce learning needs, forecasting and preparing for training needs, and identifying performance problems. They must understand what people need to perform their jobs. They must be able to assess the capabilities of the organization as a whole and identify what is needed or missing.

5. Delivery systems

L&D professionals need to assess, design and implement effective training delivery systems as well as effective learning environments. In short, they must be able to manage the learnscape. They need to be able to develop systems that are easily understood and implemented in a work environment.

6. Innovation

L&D professionals need to be able to conceptualize, design, develop and apply new learning interventions to business capability needs, while at the same time modelling strong values and openness to change.

7.   Drive

They need to demonstrate energy and enthusiasm for training programmes and informal learning initiatives and overcome the barriers people within the organization may have regarding training or learning, wherever it takes place.

Learning and the bottom line

It's critical to get feedback on the changes in the organization. This can be used to build learning strategies and improve how learning programmes are used to address business challenges.

CEOs recognize the connection between a strong learning-orientated environment and company profitability and employee motivation. For that connection to work, all the organization's leaders must participate in establishing and maintaining the learning environment and performance culture. Department heads, line managers and supervisors need to model a real-time learning approach in what they do every day, so that employees see the link between learning and work.

The L&D professional can be a learning and performance catalyst, but it's crucial that learning becomes part of daily management practice. Every supervisor, manager and executive must play their part in promoting and encouraging people to learn.

Learning and performance improvement programmes are most effective when they address a real business challenge, such as competition, customer service, productivity, new work processes or adopting new technology. Learning for learning's sake is a luxury that organizations can't afford.

This obviously means that L&D must be aware of the business challenges. With this awareness and a proactive approach, L&D professionals will be expected by CEOs to participate in business decision making and to apply their special knowledge of workplace learning to solving performance problems and seizing improvement opportunities.

L&D practitioners need to adapt to, and take control of, changing circumstances. One of the biggest changes is that employees themselves are deciding what they want to learn, how they want to learn it and when. They want a smörgåsbord of learning opportunities available 24/7, rather than the traditional occasional training course. They want to opportunistically graze on learning, rather than have feasts when the training department is ready to deliver.

In many organizations, bite-sized learning, support activities, coaching and mentoring are replacing many training programmes. This means that L&D practitioners have to become more adept at tailoring interventions more closely to the needs of individual employees – and the needs of the organization as a whole – as well as becoming more innovative, creative and proactive.

L&D practitioners need to consider who their stakeholders are and what they want. Stakeholder feedback on how their capability needs are being met is crucial to success. L&D must be visible to their stakeholders, and valued by them. Equally, the stakeholders must be visible to L&D, and that means more than just visible as a line item on a Learning Management System screen. If striving for better performance is the goal, then finding those who already perform well, and making that model of excellence available to others, is a core L&D task.

In effect, L&D needs to be more integrated within the business, so that it can better demonstrate the importance of investing in the capability of the people. L&D should be working with the operational departments to help them embed within their business plans the people development that needs to take place to make those plans achievable. These separate departmental L&D requirements can then be rolled up into a grand L&D plan, but this must start at the operational level.

From this it becomes obvious that line managers should be engaged with L&D more, because they will be the ones identifying the needs and drawing up the plans to deal with them. They will be proactively setting objectives within their own departments or functions and will therefore have a much greater investment in successfully attaining them.

The 70:20:10 model – a new focus for L&D

The 70:20:10 model contends that 70 per cent of learning within organizations happens informally, 20 per cent happens through other people and 10 per cent happens through formal events, such as training courses.

Of course it must be remembered that 70:20:10 is not a recipe or a ratio to aspire to. It is a lens through which we can look at organizational learning in a different way. It helps us focus on the huge proportion of learning that happens informally. In reality, the ratio will vary, depending on industry and on the experience of the learner.

The increasing interest being shown by organizations in the 70:20:10 model represents a fundamental change in the role of L&D, from producing and delivering formal learning to creating and managing environments in which learning is a part of work. It is about managing the support of people's on-the-job capability so they can perform well and produce the required outputs. Considering the impact of 70:20:10 inevitably pushes L&D thinking towards performance support and productivity. And that's a good thing, because that is what the organization and the C-suite are interested in.

L&D departments often struggle to present the 70:20:10 concept to the C-suite, because it goes against the grain of what L&D and every training manager before them has been selling to the senior team. The old pitch was that training would drive performance. And of course there are plenty of training courses that have produced a tangible increase in results that can be used as evidence that training works. So senior teams keep requesting training as the answer to poor performance. If the training course did not work, then somehow there was something wrong with the training course, so get a new provider, or dabble with accelerated learning in the classroom, or do something different in the hope the training will get better and, more importantly, produce sustainable results.

With 70:20:10 as a concept, L&D is now having to say that training is not the answer, or at least, it is not the whole answer (and maybe it never was... sorry), and this is a big shift in the message that L&D needs to give to the C-suite. We now need to say that training cannot possibly prepare people with all they need to know, because they cannot possibly remember everything we throw at them. What they forget after training leads to less-than-flawless performance of the work task, and this leads to costs for the business.

One of the realities that soon hits home, when looking at all the learning that is happening, is that most of the informal learning that takes place is messy and fragmented, and takes place in increasingly complex environments. This complexity is a product of the modern age, which is one of the biggest reasons why 70:20:10, or some equivalent model, is so important today. It is not easy, indeed probably impossible, to deal with this complexity in a formal learning event, so we are forced into ignoring it and hoping it will go away, or facing up to it and handling the learning complexity within the informal arena.

In a simple environment, you can develop models of best practice, and then train people to perform, using the models. This is still relevant today for some tasks, but the range of tasks that are amenable to this approach is shrinking. Computers, factory robots, production lines and even automatic dishwashers are doing more and more of these simple tasks. More and more workers now have a significant proportion of what they do that could be labelled as 'knowledge work', and this grows in complexity and scope every year.

The complexity and ongoing changes have an impact on what we can do by way of best practice. We can develop best practice when something is standing still long enough, but that happens less and less now. So we need to create an environment where people can react to their assigned tasks with sufficient skill to get them done sufficiently well, even if they don't do things perfectly. Perfection of execution is not mandatory.

One of the greatest skills, of course, is the skill to react to a new or changed task and figure out how to tackle it. At that point, the worker may need to reach out for extra information or support. It is the job of L&D to make sure that support is easily accessible at that moment, so the worker can create a new and effective way to deal with the task and move on.

The only way we can guarantee that an employee is capable at that moment of truth when they are faced with a novel task is to surround them with what they need at 'task time'. It is often called performance support, but a better term might be performer support. After all, L&D is supporting the performer so they are ready at task time and their response will exactly match the task requirements for successful completion.

'Ready' means that they have the base knowledge needed, and also know how to reach out to grasp whatever else they unexpectedly need. They, and only they, are in a position to improve their capability in a moment of truth. Training is to prepare the performer for the moment of truth, not to try and have them know everything they might need to know. Move the focus away from the task and onto the performer in the time and place in which they are performing. Start thinking about how you can 'guarantee' capability at the point of work.

Why would any C-suite incumbent not want performer support when it is explained to them in this way and it is obvious that not providing it hampers business outcomes? Performer support should automatically become a crucial strategic initiative. If you have workers who experience moments of need, and each mistake has measurable bottom line implications, then it seems foolhardy not to provide performer support in the moment on their smartphone, or on a crib card of best practice, or in any other way they could access it easily.

Find a critical process that requires flawless performance and then, after mapping it, introduce performer support at critical points, making sure the support channel is appropriate to the task and the skills of the worker. Oh, and by the way, consult with the workers. They may already have something in place of which you are unaware.

Another factor that affects how often this just-in-time support is needed is the experience people have in their job. According to research, one in four people has been working for their current employer for less than a year and one in two has been employed by their organization for fewer than five years. Thinking about this through the 70:20:10 lens brings the realization that the learning they need has to take place at their workstation. It is impossible to 'complete' the training of anybody in any role. What people learned on a course a few months ago, and maybe even remember, is likely to be out of date by the time they come to use it.

Ongoing research by Robert Kelley of Carnegie Mellon University has shown that the amount of information knowledge workers believe they need to have in their heads to do their jobs properly has declined from 75 per cent in 1986 to ten per cent in 2006.

The challenge now is to help people be more effective when they are learning informally. It is about giving people the tools they need and the skills to use those tools to manage their own learning requirements in the moment. Those requirements are dictated by the individual in response to the challenges of the task in front of them.

This is very different to the traditional approach, where L&D took responsibility for deciding what people should be learning, and then provided training to achieve this.

A number of organizations across all sectors including HP, Wal-Mart, Thomson Reuters and Standard Chartered bank are using 70:20:10. This is not a passing fad, but a new way of looking at learning in organizations that will have lasting impact.

There is resistance from some people in L&D to these changes. This seems to stem from an erroneous perception that 70:20:10 means that their role and importance is reduced. After all, if they are responsible for training, and that only accounts for 10 per cent of the learning, then some feel they are almost out of a job.

Nothing could be further from the truth. If anything, the realization that performance is so dependent on informal learning greatly increases their remit. They are now responsible for the operation of the entire learnscape, not just the small part of it that represents formal training. However, they need to reach out and grasp this larger role. It won't just be given to them.

Talk the language of business

Imagine having a CEO who understood the value of learning so completely you never had to fight over the importance of L&D to the organization's future. Think how refreshing it would be to have a CEO who was so supportive of the learning function that the value it delivered was never questioned. Consider the difference it would make if your CEO were a champion of learning in your organization.

It is entirely possible for that to happen, but only if you can overcome the miscommunication that blights many L&D relationships with the C-suite. To do that, you need to understand what causes the miscommunication, overcoming the problem by gathering the right information and presenting it in a way that will guarantee buy-in from all the organization's stakeholders (not just the CEO).

L&D must speak the language of the boardroom in order to be understood by the board. For those in L&D who teach communications skills, this is basic stuff, and yet so few do it.

Most professionals working in L&D-related departments (training, human performance technology (HPT), instructional design (ID), organizational development (OD) and HR ought to understand the logic and language of business and the organization in which they work, but most do not, say Lynn Kearny and Kenneth H. Silber, authors of "*Organizational Intelligence*".[93]

After running workshops and courses involving 2,000 HR/training professionals, the pair found that fewer than 20 per cent could answer very basic business questions about the organizations for which they worked (either in house or as consultants). They did not know about the strategic issues facing the organization, and about how they, as L&D, HR or training practitioners, contributed to the organization's bottom line (or even what the bottom line was or how it was calculated).

"Few know where to find documentation about what the business is doing, what its plans and challenges are, and how it is measuring up (including documentation that is public and required by the government)," they said.

Not understanding key business concepts or the business language stakeholders use, means L&D can't understand the organization's most urgent concerns, so their stakeholders are likely to dismiss their recommendations as naive.

"Without business intelligence, it's difficult for HR to influence business decisions or to gain the time and attention of the people who make those decisions…

"If we don't understand the business concepts and the business language our clients use, how can we understand their most pressing problems? If we make recommendations that do not take the big business issues that clients face into account, how can they trust our recommendations?"

They say L&D must understand:

- The opportunities and threats the organization faces from factors in its own industry and general economic trends
- How the organization makes a profit and achieves growth
- The purpose of the organization, the direction it is moving in and its plans for getting there (including the organization's culture)

- How the organization locates, acquires and keeps customers
- How the organization's products or services appeal to customers, how they are different from other organizations' products or services, and the company's external image
- How the organization creates, produces and delivers its products or services
- How the organization's infrastructure works.

L&D professionals also need to persuade decision-makers in the organization that L&D and its learning initiatives bring value and create results. To do that, L&D needs to:

- Communicate more strategically with the organization's key decision-makers
- Present the business case for learning in a persuasive manner that decision-makers understand
- Position L&D, not as a service provider, but as a strategic partner
- Talk about the value of training and learning in a way that businesspeople understand and respect
- Use numbers and statistics to strengthen its case
- Get support for the existing and future learning initiatives through the organization
- Communicate the value of the business-level results learning has produced.

This is not a list of 'nice to have' qualities – it's a survival list. L&D veterans Tony Bingham and Tony Jeary say L&D professionals need a set of communication strategies, skills, techniques and tools that will allow them to shine in the more demanding roles that await them.[94]

"Those who develop the requisite knowledge, communication skills and business acumen will survive and thrive in the competitive marketplace of the 21st century. Those who don't, won't."

All too often, they say, when programmes are perceived as useless or irrelevant, it's not because they were bad, but rather that the learning practitioner responsible for the programme failed to convince both superiors and learners of its practical value in terms of contribution to the organization's stated mission, strategies and objectives.

"In other words, the programme failed because it wasn't presented correctly."

Given the vast amount of communications (including formal and informal presentations, briefings, meetings, face-to-face conversations, telephone conversations, emails, memos, reports and so on) that take place in an organization, it's not surprising that inaccuracies and misunderstandings occur.

Unfortunately, unless addressed, these inaccuracies and misunderstandings can multiply.

Effective communication is a core element of organizational success in the 21st century, and training plays a large part in the overall communication practices in any organization. After all, learning professionals deal mostly with the flow of information through people, technology and the organization.

"The information they manage affects the capabilities and competiveness of the organization, as well as the quality of the leadership, the strength of the culture, and the ultimate sustainability of the enterprise," they write.

Understand the organization

To deliver the value that agile organizations need, it's vital that L&D professionals develop a deep understanding of the organization through studying available material (annual reports, press releases and so on), conversations with co-workers and colleagues, as well as interviews and observation. Not only will this give the L&D professional an understanding of the organization's business strategies, including how information flows (or does not flow) through it, but also evidence of where learning opportunities are most needed.

They need to

1. Determine the skills (knowledge, skills, judgement and attitude) that must be developed to deliver on the organizational strategy.
2. Determine the most effective way of encouraging, instructing, facilitating or supporting learners in their acquisition of these skills.

It comes down to understanding the organization and thinking like a chief executive. According to a 2010 global report from McKinsey & Company, when senior executives are involved in setting the capabilities agenda, companies are more successful, both at aligning those agendas with the capability most important to performance and at building the needed skills.[95]

"When senior leaders set the training agenda, capability building is more often explicitly linked to immediate business goals than when other groups do so," the report points out.

"For example, 38 per cent of respondents at companies whose senior leaders are involved in setting the training agenda say their company's key training and skill development programmes are focused on building or maintaining the company's number one skill priority, compared with 28 per cent at companies where HR sets the agenda."

The report concluded that companies need to be more deliberate in identifying which capabilities truly impact business performance so they can align their training programmes accordingly. This means that L&D professionals need to be more deliberate in their understanding.

What are the critical skills and capabilities?

The best way to determine the key skills and the most effective way of nurturing them is to build up information by systematic investigation.

Below are questions to ask a CEO after you have done your research and have an understanding of the organizational issues with which he or she is grappling.

- How can workplace learning contribute to meeting the challenges of our company?
- What types of workplace learning programmes would you like to see in the future?
- What abilities are most important for L&D people?
- How can I help you realize the organization's strategic objectives?
- What are the biggest human performance problems in our organization?
- What are the biggest opportunities for improving human performance?
- What one effort could we launch that might have the biggest positive impact on the performance of people in our organization?
- If we designed and developed such a learning effort, how do you think we should plan and organize for it? Who should do that? How?

- What do you think my group should do to help with the continuing implementation of the effort? What should operating managers or supervisors do? What should we do to help make sure that the effort is implemented as intended?
- What should we do to communicate our successes and our areas for improvement as the learning effort is implemented?
- How do you think we should try to keep people enthused about the change?
- What do you think we should measure to assess the relative success of the learning effort?
- How should we measure it? Who should get that feedback, and how often should they get it?

Ask business leaders to identify the knowledge and skills required to deliver value in their different departments.

- What is the nature of the business? How do you compete?
- Are there particular groups of the workforce which are critical to business value? Is there a critical cluster of workers? What knowledge and skills do they need?
- How are these key skills acquired? Is it through external recruitment, recruitment from within or training?
- If they are trainable or learnable skills, how are they trained or learned?
- To what extent do you compete on knowledge or skills? How does learning and training add strategic value?
- Looking to the future, what do you see changing on the business skills front?

From the answers, create a learning and development plan.

- Ask learners what their learning preferences are.
- Find out how people acquire or develop skills, bearing in mind that this is probably different to the answer they will give if asked.

How do members of the workforce acquire the skills necessary to do their jobs?

- Study for academic qualifications
- Study for technical or vocational qualifications
- Attend a formal training course

- Be coached or mentored by line managers
- Be coached or mentored by an external coach or mentor
- Job shadow
- Study manuals, books, videos, CD-ROMs or online material
- Access information from the internet
- Watch and listen to others at work
- Do the job on a regular basis
- Do activities unrelated to work
- Trial and error
- In-house development programmes
- On the job training
- Attend a conference, workshop or event
- Attend a professional networking event.

The most important job for L&D people is to understand the organization's vision, strategy and objectives as thoroughly as corporate-level management, so that L&D can provide value to the organization through learning and development initiatives that help make the CEO's vision a reality.

The idea is to look for ways to help the CEO and top level management achieve their goals, as well as ways learning can be used to boost strengths, shore up weaknesses and add value to the organization.

Once L&D professionals have identified the organization's core strategies and objectives, they should investigate a specific strategy with senior management. The questions they should ask senior management include:

- What needs to happen to make this strategy a reality?
- What are the barriers to this strategy?
- How can L&D help overcome those barriers?
- What are the key measures for this strategy?
- Who is responsible for carrying out this strategy?
- Does the organization have the skills or capabilities to deliver on this strategy?
- Are the right people in the right places and do they have the right skillsets?
- When will the new skills and capabilities be needed?
- Will processes need to be changed?
- Will this involve new technology, and will that require training?

- What are the organization's strengths and weaknesses?
- Is there a way to leverage those strengths to improve learning?
- Will learning help to overcome those weaknesses?
- What would happen if L&D was not involved?

All these discussions with the business must be done using terminology that the business stakeholders understand and use every day. People are pressed for time, so L&D needs to get good at writing concise and clear reports and proposals that are similar to the sort of proposals that business leaders evaluate regularly. The proposals need to focus on the business benefits and resultant organizational value, rather than the learning methodology. Think of this as talking about outputs rather than inputs. Above all, L&D people need to understand how their stakeholders define success, and how they will measure it.

Seeking budget

One area that causes a lot of wringing of hands amongst L&D people is when they need to approach the C-suite to get budget signed off for their plans. They go cap in hand to the board and try to make a case for budget to do training and some other development initiatives, such as coaching or e-learning. They seem to find it hard to make a case that is compelling enough for purse strings to be loosened for them and their needs.

It is not that the board members don't care; it is just that they are not seeing L&D as a priority. It is in part the way that L&D presents the case, and there is also often a historical perspective which has caused some scepticism of the L&D function in the minds of many CEOs. Training was sold as a performance enhancer, and then so was e-learning. Some of this works, but a lot has not produced the results promised. CEOs still see less-than-capable performance from employees doing their jobs, despite the fact they are supposed to have been trained to be able to do those jobs.

Here is a thought experiment...

You want to drive from London to Edinburgh by car. Your mechanic gets wind of this plan and rings you up. He saw your car last week outside the pub and he also knows its history. He says that it simply won't make the journey. It needs a new part on the exhaust and two new tyres. And he also says that if you end up getting delayed, you will need to drive at night so you need a new headlamp unit. In his opinion, you will be lucky to get more than 100 miles with your car in the state it is in. It certainly won't get to Edinburgh, which is almost 400 miles.

He says he can fix the car up sufficiently to get to Edinburgh for £300 and he will need it in his workshop for a day. He can't do it until next week, so that will delay your plans by a couple of days. But you really want to use your car.

What do you do?

Very few of us would ignore the mechanic and set out on a journey that is probably doomed to failure and could even be dangerous. Worst case would be if one of those worn tyres were to burst on the way. Or even if all that were to happen is that the damaged exhaust fell off, you would be stuck with a costly vehicle recovery bill.

If your car is the only option and you really do want to drive it to Edinburgh, you will pay the mechanic to get it fixed and then set off on your journey with a lot more confidence. Things could still go wrong, of course, but you have done what you can to mitigate the risk.

Why do we pay the mechanic what he asks?

Because we trust his judgement in his area of expertise. We assume the journey is not possible if he says it is not. And we trust him when he says the car is now in good enough condition to set out on the journey.

Let's apply this to asking for L&D budget.

Your board has a mission. It is to 'drive to Edinburgh'. The organization is their vehicle. It is what will carry them on their mission to 'Edinburgh'. And you, the L&D professional, are the mechanic.

You find out about the mission, and you know the vehicle won't make it safely. What do you say to the board, and how do you say it?

The mechanic did not come to you cap in hand asking/pleading for some money to fix your car. He simply said it is not fit for the journey, and he can fix it, but it will cost £300.

Now, how will you approach the board to tell them their vehicle is not fit for the journey they intend to take it on?

How will you tell them that without investing £xx,xxx in their vehicle, their mission will fail?

Worst case: their mission fails badly; the vehicle crashes and is written off, and many people lose their jobs, including the board members.

To be the 'mechanic', you need to know what the board is planning – what their mission is. You need to assess what development needs are required so people are capable of making the journey. You need the board to trust that your assessments are correct and they need to see you as key expertise that takes a lot of the risk out of their planned journey.

That might sound like a big ask, but unless you work your way into that position of trust, you will find budget hard to come by, no matter how hard you plead.

Chapter 6

Practical things for you to do

"It's critical that training and development professionals not go overboard with command and control when they support informal learning. If they do they are likely to kill it. And since informal learning makes up the bulk of learning inside organizations, this could be a truly perilous move."

Patti Shank, Director of Research at The eLearning Guild

There are several initiatives that organizations can take to enhance the informal learning that already happens in the workplace, but before doing anything, you need to build up a picture of what informal learning is already going on within your organization. Although informal learning might not have been officially sanctioned, it will definitely be happening and the methods will be constantly changing as new topics, experts and technologies emerge.

The best way to find the answers is to track the information flows, because information is the lifeblood of learning.

Find out how information moves

It's important you discover what is going on, because not all informal learning results are 'good' – some of the activities can be inefficient and the information can be inaccurate, particularly if employees are using unverified external sources. If an employee shares incorrect information with colleagues, the results can be detrimental.

So you need to determine:

- What resources do workers use; where do they turn to first, and then where do they go next? What is their default pattern to solve a problem?
- What are the differences in informal learning between new employees and experienced people?
- Do people get frustrated when they can't find what they want? Why? What do they do then? Do they give up and shove the problem away or do they go somewhere else?
- Are there departmental differences?
- Are there differences in computer access and/or computer literacy?
- Are there ad hoc repositories of information squirreled away by workers?
- What is culturally acceptable and what is not? In one culture, looking up information on the web is regarded as enterprising and the right thing to do. In another, surfing the web is seen as skiving.

You can use focus groups, interviews and questionnaires, although these should always be used with caution. If you measure something, or are even just perceived to be measuring it, people will change their behaviour based on what they think the targets might be. They will often give the answers they think are wanted, or which best suit their agenda.

Observation and casual conversation are always the best methods, although they are more time-intensive. When you research this way, you can explain that you are just trying to find out what is going on and how you can help, and reassure people that you are not 'measuring' anything.

When you are talking to people, be careful about using the word 'learning', because people don't typically think of learning as something that occurs during their day-to-day work. Typically, they associate 'learning' with something that happens when they sit in a classroom or complete an e-learning module. Until they understand what you mean by the word learning in its wider definition, it is probably best to avoid it.

Instead, use questions like "Where do you find out about 'XYZ'?" or "How do you know what to do if the widget machine fails?" or "What is the first thing you do when ABC happens?" Focus on the behaviours they use as a response to the need for information when they hit a stumbling block with a task or a project that they are involved with. This will give you an insight into employees' attitudes towards finding out information or dealing with problems. Are they engaged enough to push at barriers between them and the information they need, or do they give up easily if the information is not readily available?

Sometimes, people will give you an answer they think you want to hear. They might say something like, "Oh, I look at the intranet." Perhaps they really do, but question it further. Ask; "Is that really true? Is that where you look? Where do you go? What do you like about the navigation and search? What don't you like? What happens here if you get this particular problem? Which other websites do you use frequently?"

Also ask about the stories people tell about work and who tells them. Who do they listen to in the lunch room because they always have something interesting or useful to say? Ask people who are good at work tasks where and how they figured out how to do the task so well. Ask the new hires where they found out about things they need to know.

Ask them what they are doing differently this week to last week and why the change in how they tackle a task. This can be a gentle way to introduce the concept of ongoing learning so they start to understand how pervasive it really is. Of course, some people will get this immediately and often they will be the people who seek learning as a fundamental part of their personality, but it is surprising how many people don't realize how much they learn on a day-to-day basis.

As people open up about where and how they find out things, also ask how that process could be made easier for them. Ask about what they did in other jobs or previous companies that they wish they could do here. If you are lucky, you will find some quick wins and things that you can implement immediately to make access to information easier for people.

You will see patterns emerge, but be careful and don't jump to conclusions. Just because one method is commonly used, this does not mean it's the best one.

Part of your output from this process should also be a map of the types of information that people need, and when they need it. Do the problems that people need to solve break down into groups? Is the search for information just related to problems, or is it more general?

Another part of the output is a map of the information channels. Where does information come from and how easily does it flow? How critical is the information to operations? You'll be able to identify how information gets into the learnscape; where it comes in, and who's involved with that traffic. You need to assess the complexity of the information coming in and whether it's biased towards technical skills, personal, or clinical, or something else, depending on the industry. In other words, is there a predominance of a certain type of information that's coming in informally?

Take note, too, of how much employees rely on formal learning situations. Can they book themselves onto a formal training course? Is this easy or difficult to do? Find out how many people take up the offer of formal training methods (workshops, courses, e-learning and so on). Determine if this information occurs 'just in time', that is, little delay between request and fulfilment, or whether there is usually a big gap. Is it 'at the desk' or do people absent themselves from the workplace to take part in these formal training sessions.

You will discover if there are departmental differences within your organization. You will also discover the real communications network that exists, and this will usually bear little resemblance to the organization's hierarchical chart.

Consider unconventional methods, such as job-readiness reviews and peer appraisals, to reveal what is being learned in your organization. Track informal learning by keeping individual and departmental logs that answer questions about what is being learned, who is helping individuals to learn, and how they apply what they've learned. Ask managers to report regularly, not only on business metrics, but also on what their groups have discovered. Suggest that team supervisors operate some kind of 'learning log' for their team, where people can record the things they have discovered that help them do a better job. A competitive element could be incorporated into this, with the team rating the 'learning' with stars, and a monthly winner and a certificate of recognition for the employee who brought the most new ideas and valuable learnings into the team.

Be careful in your surveys, however, since people can express preferences to general categories of learning without understanding what that category means. An IDC report found, for example, that classroom training was twice as popular amongst learners as any other, but when this was explored deeper, the learners' view of the ideal 'classroom' did not resemble the majority of such occasions.[96] It was more like peer-to-peer learning, with individual access to experts.

Once you have compiled the information (manually or with the help of a software programme, which we'll explore in a moment), you should have a better picture of the way information does or does not flow within your organization.

You might find that certain departments don't communicate at all, which could have major implications for your organization. For example, you might discover that the marketing department doesn't communicate in a meaningful way with the production team. This means that while the marketing team might be busy promoting a special discount to generate more sales, the production team could be unaware it might be facing a sudden rise in demand as a result.

You need to determine whether your organization has key information hubs and whether the people at the centre of such hubs are subject matter experts or collators of information.

Your quest is to find out how information enters your organization's learnscape or passes through it, from one area to another. You need to determine whether the information is generated internally within the learnscape or sourced externally.

The map of information flow does not need to be totally accurate; it is more important to have qualitative rather than quantitative information about what is already going on within the organization. Once you have this benchmark, you 'measure' any changes as you implement informal learning and collaboration initiatives.

Monitor and refine

You need to measure both what you are doing and what you are getting in return. This is obviously critical if you are seeking or justifying budget.

A lot of your measurement will be subjective and anecdotal, especially in the early days. It will be about how people are reacting and engaging. It will involve talking to them and observing.

You need to monitor and refine your activities. When you have made some kind of change, ask yourself, "What did it achieve, if anything? Did we go forwards or backwards? Was it useful or not? Which departments did it work in; where didn't it work?"

Monitoring and measuring has to be a continual process. Ask for feedback. Talk to people. The more you do that, the more people will get used to those kinds of conversations and they'll volunteer the information. They will know you're interested in what they're doing and how they're getting on.

Also look outside your organization. What is going on with technology that could be used? What are others doing, now that informal learning is on the agenda of so many more organizations? Could any of it be useful? Are there groups or forums you could attend to share ideas? Follow the phrase 'informal learning' on Twitter and see what is going on there.

How people collaborate in an organization

It's becoming increasingly obvious that organizations need employees to connect and collaborate with each other. Indeed, without internal employee networks, it becomes difficult for organizations to achieve their strategic goals.

Most executives understand the importance of worker collaboration. They know that relationships are critical for obtaining information, solving problems and learning how to work. Nearly 80 per cent of the senior executives surveyed in a 2005 study said that effective coordination across product, functional and geographic lines was crucial for growth.[97] Yet only 25 per cent of the respondents described their organizations as 'effective' at sharing knowledge across boundaries.

Many companies have invested considerable funds, time and energy in promoting a collaborative workplace and in collaborative software, but find that their technology at best fails to deal with the underlying problem and at worst becomes a source of information overload that undermines effective collaboration. It's often unclear whether efforts to enhance networks promote productive collaboration or just consume money and time, according to Robert L. Cross and Roger D. Martin, experts in employee collaboration.[98]

Frequently, employers are unaware of the real employee networks that exist in their organization, since the real work patterns often bear little relationship to the organizational chart. A typical organizational chart shows relations between people within an organization. It might include managers to workers, directors to managing directors, chief executive officer to various departments and so forth.

"Put an organizational chart in front of most employees, from line workers to executives, and they will tell you that the boxes and lines do not really capture the way work gets done in their organization," say social network experts Rob Cross and Andrew Parker.[99] Employees create their own informal social networks. While they often don't appear on organizational charts, very little of value is accomplished without them.

These networks are dynamic entities that can be fragmented by bad management decisions or uninformed organizational restructuring. For example, the launch of an incentive programme by senior management may inadvertently result in less, not more collaboration, when employees in different departments realize their collaborators are now also their competitors.

Employee networks are often prone to disconnections, which can occur due to lack of physical proximity, or to fragmentation between departments, functions or hierarchy. These breaks can undermine the achievement of important organizational objectives.

Social network analysis

Social network analysis (also called 'organizational network analysis') is a crucial tool for revealing who is connected to whom within an organization. It maps and measures relationships and flows between people, groups, organizations, computers and other information/knowledge processing entities.[100]

It also allows people to identify how best to interact to share knowledge. It can be used to:

- Visualize relationships inside and outside the organization

- Help identify who knows who and who might know what – teams and individuals playing central roles, thought leaders, key knowledge brokers, experts and so on
- Pinpoint isolated teams or individuals
- Identify knowledge bottlenecks
- Work strategically to improve knowledge flows
- Accelerate the flow of knowledge and information across functional and organizational boundaries
- Improve the effectiveness of formal and informal communication channels
- Raise awareness of the importance of informal networks.

The process of social network analysis (SNA) typically involves the use of questionnaires and/or interviews to gather information about the relationships within a defined group or network of people. The responses are then mapped using an SNA software tool (such as NetDraw, Pajek or UCINET). Once the data has been gathered and analysed, it's then possible to plan and prioritize the appropriate changes and interventions to improve the social connections and knowledge flows within the group or network.

The key stages of the SNA process will usually include the following:

- Identifying the network of people to be analysed (such as a team, group or department)
- Interviewing managers and key staff to understand the specific needs and problems
- Clarifying objectives, defining the scope of the analysis and agreeing on the level of reporting required
- Formulating questions, developing the survey methodology and designing a questionnaire
- Surveying the individuals in the network to identify the relationships and knowledge flows between them
- Using a software mapping tool to visually map out the network
- Reviewing the map and the problems and opportunities highlighted
- Designing and implementing actions to bring about desired changes
- Mapping the network again after a suitable period of time.

According to Cross and Parker, the best way to check the results is to measure increases in collaboration in light of how well the group has achieved relevant performance objectives.

They also suggest enhancing worker connectivity by convening bonding activities, such as company meetings, off-site employee gatherings and strategic planning workshops and retreats. To help workers to get to know each other and thus increase the opportunity for closer collaboration, organizations should provide an attractive site within the office where employees can meet over lunch or breaks.

Boosting revenue and productivity using network analysis

It's now also possible to map and analyse the value in terms of revenue and productivity that is created or destroyed in employee networks. To make these network analysis tools more useful, executives must reorientate them toward the revenue and productivity benefits that collaborative interactions generate, the costs such interactions impose, and opportunities to improve connectivity at the points that create the greatest economic value.

In 'Mapping the value of employee collaboration', Robert L. Cross et al [101] gave the case of a biotechnology company that relied on sharing best practices among quality control engineers to help its manufacturing facilities increase the production of new products. Using network analysis, the company could see which engineers took part in interactions that produced time savings and the greatest and lowest cost, respectively.

The results from the network analysis tools had been aggregated to reveal the economic value created through interactions across locations in the network, to identify where collaborative breakdowns inhibited the transfer of proven practices, and to show how costly these breakdowns were. The company was then able to see where it made economic sense to invest in tools, training and team-building efforts.

To achieve similar results, organizations must first map the collaborative networks and then analyse the economic benefits and costs that key interactions within those networks create. Interventions can include replicating high performance networks, training employees to emulate the collaborative efforts of successful colleagues, making expertise and advice more readily available and overhauling performance metrics. Such interventions can help companies to reduce complexity, redefine roles, serve customers and clients more effectively and allocate financial, physical and human resources more efficiently.

The real value comes when companies move from mapping interactions to quantifying the benefits and costs of collaboration. To do so, companies must assess the time employees spend on interactions of various types, as well as the savings and sales contributions of specific collaborations.

The report gave the example of an engineering company which was experiencing growing pains as international expansion made it increasingly difficult to bring together construction managers and engineers, whose objectives were frequently in conflict (the former focused on cutting costs, the latter on technical solutions). "Unfortunately, the company's linear view of the construction process – emphasizing the tasks performed by each group and the handoffs between them – shed little light on collaborative issues," the researchers reported.

Network analysis of one of the engineering company's high-performing groups showed that a small number of construction managers and engineers accounted for 35 per cent of all the collaboration occurring within it. This kind of collaboration dramatically enhanced the group's ability to deliver expertise. Identifying and building connectivity between specialists in other groups helped the firm to raise its construction revenue from $80 million to $275 million in a single year.

"Targeted action is dramatically more effective than promoting connectivity indiscriminately, which typically burdens already-overloaded employees and yields network diseconomies. A more informed network perspective helps companies to identify the few critical points where improved connectivity creates economic value by cutting through business unit and functional silos, physical distance, organizational hierarchies, and a scarcity of expertise."

Don't discard formal learning

Both formal and informal learning have important roles to play in the workplace. Training, for example, is necessary for bringing novices up to speed, says Jay Cross.[102] "You don't learn algebra by standing around the water cooler talking with your pals," he says.

"Changes in the world, especially in technology, ensure that we're all novices at some things. Training and certification are mandated for compliance. Training is standard for on-boarding new hires and grooming managers, although it's better when supplemented with job rotations, coaching, and plain old walking around. Push learning is often the most effective way for a newcomer to master the lay of the land, the jargon, the cheat sheets, and sacred knowledge, and to be recognized for it.

"Not that formal learning is bad. Learning that is purely self-directed doesn't help people who don't know what they need to know. At times, others know what's good for you and push you beyond what's familiar and comfortable."

There are times, he says, when an organization identifies an area for improvement or a new priority, and pushing workers through a learning experience can be expedient and productive.

"Learners are not instructional designers and may not naturally come up with the optimal way to acquire a new skill," he adds.

Just because we now realize how much of the learning at work is happening informally, this does not in any way reduce the importance of formal learning. There is a synergy between the two and you could say that a lot of the informal learning that happens is only possible when formal learning has first provided a basic framework of knowledge. That framework can also be a standardized base of knowledge which each employee must have to function in their role.

The skill required from L&D professionals lies in understanding when a formal learning intervention is appropriate, and when it is not. There is an assumption, often held by L&D professionals, and their internal 'clients' and learners, that every learning and development requirement is best addressed by a course. Learning must be approached from a much wider perspective and one way to do this is through the lens of the 70:20:10 model referred to earlier.

In many blogs and magazines, informal learning is touted as a 'better' way to learn. I think this is misleading, because good formal training is an excellent tool, when used for the right purpose in the right context. First consider the need, and then decide on the tool for the job. There is an oft-used quote from Abraham Maslow "if all you have is a hammer, everything looks like a nail". Unfortunately, many L&D professionals only know about formal training; it is their hammer and their solution of choice.

It is also unfortunate that many people see informal learning and formal learning as opposites that are mutually exclusive, so they will at times 'choose sides' and debate which is the better way. Extremism is seldom the answer to complex areas, including human development. Instead, always consider the desired outcome in order to choose the right tool. As an example, let's look at how this applies to an e-learning system.

Know it versus find it

Think about what you want users to achieve from an e-learning system that provides knowledge and information to users. It is probably something like:

- Users can do their job
- Users can do their job better
- Users have better interpersonal skills
- Users can pass an exam for regulatory purposes
- Users can get information in the moment to solve problems
- Users can handle conflict and disagreement better
- Users can diagnose and troubleshoot the new product.

Your outcomes will be specific to your organization, to each user, and probably dovetail into much wider change initiatives within your overall employee learning and development plans.

Now consider how the users would use an online information system in order to achieve your outcomes. You will find that the style of use will fall into two broad camps, Know It and Find It, or somewhere on a continuum between them.

Know it: absorb information and learn it so that it is available via memory recall in the future, without recourse to the original information.

Find it: access information that will help solve a problem now, so employees can complete a task assigned to them.

One catchy way this fundamental difference in function has been described is 'just-in-case' versus 'just-in-time'. This, in a nutshell, is the simple KiFi model.

This model has a number of implications that are vitally important to anybody specifying, designing, purchasing or promoting the use of a computer-based information resource.

Form follows function

Consider the old design adage that "form follows function". When designing something, be it a building, a vehicle or an online system, you need to first consider the function, and only then create a design that will enable the product to fulfil its purpose, its function.

Think of how a car differs from a truck. Although they are both types of motorized transport, they differ in form due to their different functions. They are different in size, style, shape, power and also have different human/machine interfaces (the controls that the driver uses, for example). There are many similarities, but also key differences, because the principal function of each is different.

In the same way that you can look at a truck and recognize it as a truck rather than a car because of specific aspects of its design, you can do this with Know it and Find it systems. You should be aware, however, that there are no naming conventions that system suppliers will follow, so you need to be able to do this for yourself.

You also need to recognize systems that have been designed without adequately considering their function, or designed without a clear function in mind, or have ended up being some kind of hybrid that does neither function well.

So, given their functions of Know it or Find it, what does the form of a good system look like?

There are many ways they will be similar, in the same way a car and a truck will both have steering wheels. Similarities for good systems will be things such as highly credible content authors, appealing on-screen design, with fonts and colours selected for readability and high comprehension, available both on and off line and across different platforms, simple and quick navigation and so on. Ignore these similarities for the moment and concentrate on the differences.

So when you look at a system, what are you looking at? Is it a Know it system or a Find it system? Or one that has been built without following that age-old design maxim that form follows function?

User motivation

One area where the form of a system must be congruent with the function is user motivation; a very hot topic for these types of system. Now that you have the KiFi model to help, it is much easier to sort out what is going on.

When users need to go through online modules to embed information and learning (Know it), and there is no clear and immediate need perceived by them to learn the information, results are typically poor. It's an accepted learning theory that adults learn best when there is some urgency and that they are motivated to learn through their own need, rather than an imposed requirement.

It becomes obvious that the online Know it course itself must provide motivation and user engagement, if it is to be in any way successful. Good courses cater for this with lots of 'seductive augmentation' – extras to engage the learner, and then keep them engaged throughout a module. This is often done with games, extra pictures and 'eye candy', such as video stories with interesting scenarios and, more recently, full-blown participatory games that follow the style of those available on gaming consoles.

But even with all of this, busy users with full in-trays will not willingly invest time in learning something just in case they might need it one day. They will, however, invest time in finding information that will solve a pressing problem or question and help them deal with their full in-tray. That information might be pure data, such as a tax code, or it could be a principle of employment law, or how to do something, or how to apply the data they just found.

Users will typically only access a Find it system when they actually need some information at that moment. Before they even click the mouse, they have an intrinsic motivation to use the system and find out what they need to know.

Thus there is no need for any of the extras that have the role of seductive augmentation to engage and motivate; in fact, if they are there, the extras often get in the way of finding the information needed.

Think of your own experience when trying to find information on the internet. Which sites offer you the best experience when you are simply looking for information?

I am sure you can relate to this quote from Tim Berners-Lee, the inventor of the internet. "Web users ultimately want to get at data quickly and easily. They don't care as much about attractive sites and pretty design."

Define your ideal KiFi positioning

If you bought a car to do a truck's job, you would probably fail to do your task. The same logic applies to Know it and Find it systems. If you buy the wrong system to do a job, you will probably fail to get the job done.

You need to decide, given your outcomes, which genre of system will be needed. And note that this is not necessarily an either/or decision. You may end up recognising that you need both types of system to fulfil your outcomes. There is nothing wrong with having both a car and a truck.

Your first step is to define what you want in terms of function, and to do this you need to start with a list of the outcomes you expect or want from a system. This needs to be a numbered and prioritized list. If you do not yet have a list of outcomes, then you MUST start by making one, either on your own or, preferably, with other stakeholders, including the proposed end-users.

Now plot on the KiFi line where each numbered outcome would fall in terms of its need for a Know it solution or a Find it solution to achieve the outcome. One way you can think of this is that the closer in time you bring the use of the system to the point at which the information is required, the closer you move towards a Find it system. This does not mean that there is no learning. Far from it; often, the learning will be greater when the information accessed from the system is placed immediately into context and used. You can refine this process by plotting the outcomes above or below the line, based on their priority.

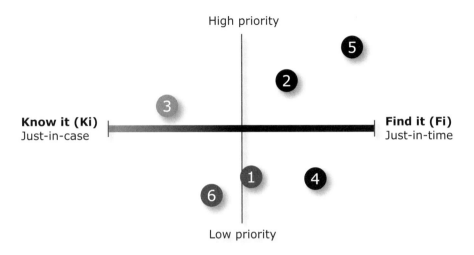

Figure 1: Example KiFi™ diagram with plotted outcomes

Whatever your final diagram, this starts to help you define at a high level what kind of system you need, and whether you might actually need more than one system.

Multi-purpose system (KiFi spread)

It is obvious that you can use a Know it product for Find it purposes and vice versa. The question then becomes "How well can I use a particular Know it product for Find it purposes, and vice versa?"

Notice that this is just the same with the car and the truck. Up to a point, you can use a car to move cargo, and you could use a truck to commute.

So which do you need? A car, or a truck, or both?

We looked at the form of a product earlier and considered how this should be dictated by the function. Given these differences, it becomes clear that a Know it system will usually be less than ideal as a reference resource. You cannot easily flit from place to place within the often rigidly-sequenced content to follow your own path of enquiry. You can't search or skim through multi-media content for specific information, especially if you have never seen it before. Trying to find specific information within a Know it module can be very frustrating. Indeed, the very things that make for a good Know it system are the same things that cause barriers when trying to use it as a Find it system.

On the other hand, a Find it resource can score well on learning, because when it is used, the information gained is usually put into practice immediately. This practical application of new information leads to it being retained for next time, even though learning was not the original goal, which was to solve the problem. The learning derived from a Find it system is a wonderful secondary benefit beyond the initial outcome of finding information to solve a current problem.

However, the learning derived from a Find it resource will be informal and thus there will be no control over what is learnt and when, so it probably won't satisfy any specific learning outcomes, such as preparation for a Food Hygiene exam or Health & Safety test.

You need to go back to what you are seeking to achieve. What is the need of the user and thus the required function of the system?

Now you can decide on the form of a solution: Know it or Find it or both!

Market what you are doing

Setting something up is not enough. People need to find out about it – and the way you promote it is important. You need marketing.

We often assume that marketing deals only with delivering a product or service to an external customer, but the same thinking can guide you to generating awareness and encouraging use of your informal learning initiatives. Most L&D people have never had "marketing" in their job descriptions. They've never been formally trained on marketing principles, yet their new role in informal learning requires them to be effective internal marketers.

Larger organizations probably already have people who manage internal communications. They can help, but you need to be aware that internal marketing is a bit different from internal communications, which tends to be a one-way, top-down flow of information, primarily concerned with ensuring that staff have the relevant information to do their jobs correctly.

Internal marketing includes the use of persuasion and the communication of features and benefits to elicit 'buying' behaviour. If you have access to internal marketing experts, that's great; if not, get advice from people who know about external marketing, because the fundamentals are very similar.

As with most things, you need to start with your desired outcomes and get them agreed to by the senior management team. If they are not wholly in agreement about the aims, the chances of the exercise succeeding will be limited.

Get clear on your message, which might be something like: "In a world where knowledge has become increasingly perishable, people learn best through a combination of having the right knowledge in the right context with the right people. Knowing the right people to ask the right question has more power than knowing all the answers".

Once the objectives have been decided, the next step is the same as with any external marketing campaign: get to grips with the needs of the marketplace – and that requires market research.

How can you segment or divide up your market into groups? How can you reach those groups? Where do they get their information from? Whom do they trust? What issues are important to them?

I am hoping you can see that this exercise in market research can easily be combined with the exercise at the start of this chapter on finding out how information flows in your organization. Again, it is about qualitative data rather than quantitative.

Development of a marketing strategy follows the research, and then you will end up with a campaign. Note well that it must be viewed as a campaign, which has continual and persistent reinforcement. Make use of standard marketing methods, such as presentations, posters, leaflets, videos, desk drops and even a letter or message from the CEO. It is crucial to communicate in a language that relates to the audience, not the transmitter, and it is equally crucial to push the information via the social interaction channels that exist within the organization.

Talk to as many leaders as possible in your organization about the benefits of informal learning and the strategy you plan to implement. Hold lunch-and-learns and town hall meetings, and attend management meetings where you can communicate the values of informal learning. Encourage all levels of management to allow their employees time to share their knowledge. For example, they should not be too critical of people who are talking at the water cooler, because it could be informal learning in action.

Take the team supervisors aside; make them feel special and say, "We're investing in you so you can help your team perform better". This way, you will greatly increase the number of people who use what is available within the learnscape.

Have team supervisors spend time with your subject matter experts so they build their network of people who can help when they have questions or problems. There's an obvious win for them in being able to inform their team where all this good information can be found.

You could also introduce some simple incentives, such as gift vouchers or competitions, as a reward for helping others perform better in their jobs. Get creative!

As with any marketing campaign, the focus needs to be on WIIFM (What's In It For Me). It is a subtle sales job. What do the employees get in return for investing their attention, time and energy into the new informal learning initiatives? Just telling them what you are doing is not enough. They need to see how the features can provide benefits that provide them with results that they want. Ideally, their first use of a new system will result in a win for them, or in some kind of advantage. They have to be left thinking, "Wow! I can see how this could be valuable."

If they don't want what you're offering, but you know it will really help them, you've got to educate them to want it. People will be at different stages in terms of how they have structured or created their own personal learning environments. Everyone has one, but they probably don't think of it as something they have created. It is the network of people they ask about things, the places they go, such as Google, to find out information, the blogs they read, the new items they are interested in and so on. Some will already have very effective personal learning environments; most will not. How can what you are doing add to and improve the individual's personal learning environment?

How can you educate them about what you are doing and how it will solve their on-the-job challenges? Think about that last question again and notice that it is the basis for any marketing campaign.

Many learners are not self-directed; they are waiting for directions. It's time to tell them that the rules have changed. It's in their self-interest to convert from training pawns to proactive learning opportunists. You need to remind them, frequently, that learning is a continuous goal, if you are to ensure that learning is kept 'front of mind' instead of 'bottom of drawer'. How you promote that message will depend on where they are already in terms of their understanding of informal learning.

As you conduct your internal marketing campaign, notice what feedback you get about the campaign itself and the outcomes. Re-use the positive feedback within the campaign. Acknowledge and make changes as a result of the negative feedback.

Strangely enough, one of the places to promote informal learning is within your formal training programmes. The opportunities and availability of ongoing performance support continue to build knowledge and skills informally back in the workplace. This principle should be a standard part of any formal training day. As well as helping people understand what is available to them, ensure they are also taught how to use it effectively and how to be better informal learners.

Get support from subject matter experts on your staff. These are the people who are respected for their knowledge and experience. When they are asked a question, and they say "Go to 'XYZ' on the intranet, or use this online resource, or check out this industry magazine", then that will spread. It is the local internal experts who will tend to be the hubs of any marketing message that goes viral within the organization.

In many cases, you will be best starting with a specific employee community – for example, the research department or sales department – where there is a common goal and common issues. Within that community, focus on those who you think will be the early adopters.

Employee engagement

As we saw in Chapter 2, there is a direct link between learning in an organization and the level of engagement of the employees. In order for employees to seek learning, to be self-directed learners, they first need to be engaged with the vision and mission of the organization.

The level of employee engagement is part of the learnscape, because it affects learning. Thus, L&D people who want to improve the effectiveness of their learnscape need to be working on improving employee engagement.

The Chartered Institute for Personnel & Development (CIPD) defines employee engagement as "a combination of commitment to the organization and its values and a willingness to help out colleagues (organizational citizenship)".

Employee engagement is more than job satisfaction and motivation, it says. It is something the employee has to offer, but it can't be a part of an employment contract.

Research from Development Dimensions International (DDI) compared the impact that the quality of leadership has on several key dimensions, and found that organizations with high quality leadership had five times higher employee engagement when compared with organizations with low quality leadership. The results also indicated almost three times greater talent retention, over four times greater productivity, customer satisfaction and quality of services, and nearly three times greater business performance.[103] Employers want engaged employees because they deliver improved business performance.

When employers deliver on their commitments (when they fulfil their employees' expectations), they reinforce employees' sense of fairness and trust in the organization.

Organizations increasingly recognize the importance of their 'brand'. Engaged employees will help promote the brand and protect the employer from the risks associated with poor service levels or product quality, according to the CIPD. Similarly, a strong employer brand will help in attracting and retaining employees.

Blessing White surveyed 10,914 workers worldwide and found that only 31 per cent were engaged. Interestingly, this result varied depending on region: 37 per cent in India, 36 per cent in Australia/New Zealand, 33 per cent in North America, 30 per cent in Europe, 26 per cent in Southeast Asia, and only 17 per cent in China. In most regions, an additional 25 per cent were found to be "almost engaged".[104] Improving these relatively low numbers would bring real value.

Very few UK employees feel engaged. A 2010 Gallup Engagement Survey found that only 24 per cent of UK employees felt engaged with their job.[105] The CBI says employee engagement is now the biggest challenge facing employers.

Employers recognize they have a problem, however: current engagement strategies are not working.

The problem is that employers' engagement strategies focus mainly on big-picture issues, such as work/life balance and charismatic leadership, which don't address two key issues – the employee's relationship with their immediate manager and the employee's trust in the employer.

Surveys by the Training Foundation and others show that less than 20 per cent of managers have received any training in engagement skills and how to bring out the best in people. It seems that most employers don't recognize that managers need to know how to engage with and bring out the best in their people. The result? Employees are disengaged and perform poorly or they leave. Nearly three quarters of people leave their manager and not the job.[106]

An engaged workforce is critical for consistent success and is a huge competitive advantage. Disengaged workers act like an anchor, generating massive costs from things like mistakes and subsequent rework, not doing that extra little bit beyond normal clocking out time, and not bothering to report poor quality during production.

Available research, for example an APCO Worldwide Survey, shows that organizations using blogs, wikis and internal social networks enjoy an improvement in employee engagement.[107] Still, CLOs can expect to encounter sceptics – those who question the ROI or even the lack of organizational control over informal learning tools.

How to build an engaged workforce

Engagement is founded on trust – trust in the employer and in the manager. David MacLeod, co-author of a UK government report on employee engagement, said the recession has led to a general weakening of trust; this needs to be rebuilt before there can be any significant improvement in employee engagement.[108]

Engagement is driven by emotions, so employers must pay more attention to the role they play in people's decisions to engage or not.

Employers focus too much on organizational initiatives, such as flexible working, says Macleod. "These are important but are not producing significant improvements because they are outweighed by a far more influential factor. There's growing evidence that the employee/immediate manager relationship is the key factor in up to eight out of ten decisions to leave a job, the ultimate measurement of engagement."

The CIPD suggests measuring employee attitudes. Attitude survey data can be used to identify areas in need of improvement and can be combined with other data to support performance management.

The drive for an engaged workforce needs to build on good people management and development policies and the active support of line managers, it says. Those strategies and policies must be aligned with those of the organization.

It's important that employees understand how their work contributes to organizational outcomes.

There is no short cut to building and maintaining employee engagement, but the time, effort and resource required will be amply repaid by the performance benefits.

There is no definitive all-purpose list of engagement 'drivers'. However, CIPD research into employee attitudes found that the main drivers of employee engagement are:

- Having opportunities to feed your views upwards
- Feeling well-informed about what is happening in the organization
- Believing that your manager is committed to your organization.

Perceived managerial fairness in dealing with problems also impacts considerably on individual performance, although it is not significantly related to engagement.

Similarly, the Institute of Employment Studies (IES) has concluded that the main driver of engagement is a sense of feeling valued and involved. The main components of this are said to be:

- Involvement in decision-making
- Freedom to voice ideas, to which managers listen
- Feeling enabled to perform well
- Having opportunities to develop the job
- Feeling the organization is concerned for employees' health and well-being.

Engagement levels are influenced by employees' personal characteristics, and a minority of employees are likely to resist becoming engaged in their work. But people are also influenced by the jobs they do and the experiences they have at work. The way in which both senior management and line managers behave towards, and communicate with, employees, plus the way in which work is organized and jobs defined, contribute significantly towards making work meaningful and engaging.

Fundamental to managing engagement is that action is taken on the findings of attitude surveys. It is important to identify issues and communicate an action plan to employees.

Although measurement can be key to identifying issues, managing an engaged workforce also requires 'soft skills' and the creation of a culture based on mutual respect between managers and employees.

Chapter 7

More tools and ideas you can use

"Tell me and I'll forget; show me and I may remember; involve me and I'll understand"

Chinese Proverb

Informal learning takes many forms in an organization. Indeed, this is one of the reasons that people can find the whole idea a bit daunting. There is no simple formula you can apply for guaranteed success. The best you can do is influence informal learning, because you certainly cannot control it in the sense of pulling lever 'A' so that result 'B' happens. The kinds of tools and initiatives that work for your organization may not work so well somewhere else, and vice versa.

This means that I cannot give you a recipe for the ingredients and steps you need to use to bake your informal learning cake for your organization. What I can do here is give you a number of ideas and examples, in addition to the ones you have already seen earlier in the book, so you can pick and choose the ingredients, and create your own recipe. Try them out; come up with your own combinations, and find out what works for you.

As you read through the following tools and ideas, consider how you could use them in your organization to assist the information flow from where it is to where it is needed in order to produce capability at the point of work.

Collaboration and sharing

Foster a culture of cooperation rather than competition by encouraging people to share their expertise, no matter how insignificant it may seem to them, and discourage people from hoarding information. It is worth remembering the quote from Tim Sanders used earlier in the book: "Knowledge sharing is the basis of everything. Share knowledge with reckless abandon."

To reap the full benefit of social technologies, organizations must transform their structures, processes, and cultures: they will need to become more open and non-hierarchical. Ultimately, the power of social technologies hinges on the full and enthusiastic participation of employees who are not afraid to share their thoughts and trust that their contributions will be respected. Creating these conditions within your learnscape will be far more challenging than choosing the right tools, gaining management approval and implementing the technologies themselves.

It requires genuine leadership, with senior managers setting an example to their departments about how it is no longer acceptable to hoard knowledge. This is a change that many managers struggle to make, but if they don't do it themselves, they are unlikely to convince their departments of the benefits.

In the previous chapter, we talked about finding out how the information flows into and around your organization. Once you've discovered how people are collaborating informally, you need to ensure that new knowledge is discoverable and appealing for self-directed learners on a continual basis, and then provide them with the tools they need to make the process easier and more effective.

Many internal social media implementations have failed within their first few months. We have all heard the stories in which, soon after launch, the social media exchanges drop away and the atmosphere is like tumbleweed blowing through a ghost town. One reason can certainly be choosing the wrong technology platform for the desired outcomes and employee needs, but more often these failures are a result of the way the systems are implemented.

In the earlier days of social media rollouts, it was thought that the way to do it was to drive it from the ground up: to start a group using it and then let it spread virally within the organization. And indeed there have been success stories where this has happened. This has worked when there has been a clear objective and benefit for the community using the social network. It provided much more than a 'water-cooler conversation'.

Many system vendors described employee social networks as 'virtual water coolers', reinforcing the impression that this is a place for side conversations, not for real work with a real business objective.

These days, it is much less common to hear proponents of the establishment of a virtual water cooler. It is increasingly accepted that for a social network inside a company to succeed, it needs clearly-defined business objectives and approval from senior management. It needs to be a place where real work gets done, with the social environment providing richer communication and collaboration capabilities for business processes that you would have been working on anyway.

Knowledge systems

Create places where knowledge can be deposited and accessed. There are many ways to do it, some high tech and some low tech.

At the high tech end, there are things such as wikis, blogs, forums and full blown knowledge management systems. These tools are simple, single function applications that are focused on a specific problem or interaction. When these applications are combined in a common interface, a new platform for sharing knowledge is created. At the low tech end are things like pinboards with messages stuck to them.

The Cegos Group carried out an in-depth survey in March 2009 in which it compared the viewpoints of 2,355 employees and 485 HR directors/training managers from companies employing more than 500 staff in the UK, France, Germany and Spain.[109] Among the trends it identified were that learners want to see more technology-driven learning developed and that they are keen to embrace collaborative tools such as wikis, blogs and forums.

Collaboration is especially important, according to a Forrester Research report, 'The State of Collaboration Software Implementations: 2011', because today's workforce is largely decentralized. According to the report, 43 per cent of information employees work from multiple locations during the course of a month. This might be why, according to the same report, 42 per cent of respondents surveyed say they are spending more on social tools, such as blogs or wikis.

L&D tends to think there's little they can do in terms of social media and collaboration and that's a mistake, according to Clark Quinn, a learning and organizational strategist. In an article on his Learnlets blog,[110] he wrote that L&D can "make courses about how to use social media better (not everyone knows how to communicate and collaborate well), share best practices, work social media into formal learning to make it easier to facilitate a segue into the workplace. They can also provide performance support for the social media, and facilitate its use.

"They can unearth good practices in the organization and share them, foster discussion, and so on; seed, feed, weed, and breed. (And, yes, L&D interventions there will be formal in the sense that they're applying rigour, but they're facilitating emergent behaviours that they don't own.)

"This latter, the use of social media in the organization for work should happen, as that's where the continual innovation happens. As I say: optimal execution is only the cost of entry; continual innovation is the necessary competitive differentiator. Formal learning helps execution, and so does performance support, but innovation comes from social interaction. And L&D groups shouldn't leave innovation to chance. They have a role to play."

Collaborative tools allow users to share their successes and failures, says Tom Kelley, author and an expert in training and education.[111]

"Content creation tools finally exist that make it easy for anyone who is an expert to share knowledge. They work well for anyone who has experienced some success and wants to share it with partners/colleagues/employees looking for a new or different way to be successful."

With wikis, blogs, audio-over-slides, video and social networking tools, learning organizations can manage public forums where knowledge is openly shared. Peer-to-peer teaching tools require training organizations to give up some control of the content creation process, but these tools also increase the accessibility and speed with which content can be updated or corrected.

"Professionals want to learn tips, tricks and techniques from successful peers in their community. They don't really want to listen to scripted 'talent' or to professional trainers." Those tips and tricks should be brief, focused and last no more than ten minutes.

"Short, direct, and specific answers or coaching comments that teach professionals how to be successful, how to approach a situation or customer, address different vertical markets, or solve any other narrow problem are immensely impactful. They are also easily searched within a database and are much more easily updated and replaced than courses, white papers or one-hour video segments."

Decentralize content creation, says Kelly, and you will capitalize on a scalable formula for successful informal learning.

The beauty of the newer knowledge-sharing tools is the ability to monitor, track and measure their success. L&D can measure how many people are searching for specific topics, how many best practices are being shared, and how improvements are being realized in that area. It is obviously useful to know what really are the most frequently asked questions, especially those that can be addressed company-wide, and to monitor what are the results once they are answered.

"It's as if we've recorded water cooler conversations, put them in one place and have the ability to effectively respond to questions raised."

The conversations can provide real-time information about what employees need. For example, if staff constantly view or comment on a blog post on best practice for customer management, it could mean they require more training or that the current training systems in place are insufficient, says Arthur Chan of Management IQ.[112]

"To senior management, this could indicate a need to change their training provider or that the training programme needs updating," he says. Social media can provide feedback not just for the L&D department but the business as a whole.

"Ultimately, those who listen to the conversations taking place and respond appropriately will gain the most from social media," he concludes.

But social media alone is not enough, according to Josh Bersin, of Bersin & Associates.[113] Many organizations see wikis and blogs as learning solutions themselves, but his company's research shows otherwise. These tools do not necessarily create engagement or facilitate the sharing of information unless they are implemented in context. For example, many companies find that wikis fail unless they are directed toward very narrow fields of like-minded employees.

"When a wiki is dedicated to customer service professionals and organized around the precise types of problems customer service representatives see, it can be enormously powerful. Simply creating a 'company wiki', however, is more likely to be confusing and randomly used," he says.

"High-performing L&D teams understand what all of these tools do and then select the right ones for different applications."

Wikis

A wiki is a software application that allows any user to easily update web pages. Some organizations are moving to wiki-based intranets and giving up control of knowledge dissemination. This allows an intranet to develop in the ways that are most useful to employees. Resources are shared, collaboration is facilitated and employees' trust in the organization is increased.

A wiki can be collaboratively edited by readers. Wikis have resulted in the growth of communities such as Wikipedia, the free, online encyclopaedia that any user can edit and which has grown into the largest encyclopaedia in the world.

While normal corporate communication flows from top to bottom, the wiki encourages communication to flow from the bottom up.

An internal wiki at Cisco, for example, to which any employee can submit ideas, yielded more than 400 new business ideas in just 18 months, resulting in the identification of more than $3 billion in new market opportunities.[114]

Its ease of use makes a wiki a great tool for disseminating information around the world and the simplicity of editing makes it simple for employees in satellite offices to provide input back to the company's headquarters. It also provides a way for teams with members in different locations to work together and share information on a project. It's a perfect tool for small teams of people who need to create and distribute information to a large number of readers.

A wiki can also enhance or even replace meetings. IBM, for example, held a global wiki meeting in September 2006. Over 100,000 people from more than 160 countries took part in the three-day brainstorming session.

Blogs

Blogs (web logs) are user-generated websites in which entries are made in a journal style and displayed in chronological order. Each entry can be tagged with keywords (for example, informal learning) to make them searchable and, therefore, easier to find.

Like wikis, they are another valuable way for employees to share ideas and information, comment on developments within the industry and so on. They're easy to update and virtually eliminate the need for printed versions of information.

There are several different types of organizational blogs, including internal blogs, event blogs, product blogs and CEO blogs. Internal blogs are being developed, for example, to disseminate news within organizations.

RSS feeds

RSS, the most common type of feed, allows individuals to have all the information from all the feeds that they subscribe to in one place. This saves the individual the time of going from website to website to find information. Because the user selects what feeds they want to subscribe to, there is no spam.

RSS feeds are an effective way to monitor a large amount of content in a short amount of time. A feed reader is required to put the feeds in one place and enable viewing of them all. These feeds can be received through mobile phones, pagers, other mobile devices, and laptop and desktop computers.

Forums and message boards

Unlike blogs, which are more of an online journal or diary, where the visitor can read material and then leave a comment or feedback, online message boards and forums promote a lively exchange of ideas and opinions. They encourage interaction, since users can post messages and questions, aimed at eliciting responses from other users. Besides a company-wide forum, organizations can also set up forums for people who work in the same department but different geographic locations, who are working on a specific project, or who've attended a training programme.

Make it easy to access. Remember, once learners have hit a barrier when searching for information, they won't go back and use the system again – they'll try to find another place to get the same information.

An important point to bear in mind is that the more formal knowledge management systems get, and the more company-owned, the harder it will be to get people to use them.

The following story, which may even be true, illustrates the danger of interfering with a popular knowledge management system...

There is a story about a power company where there was an old battered exercise book. This was held behind the counter at a café outside the main depot where most of the line workers stopped for lunch or a coffee after their shifts. People would ask for the book, scribble some notes in it, and then hand it back. The company found out about the notebook, in which were lots of tips and tricks that would be really useful for any new line worker. With a great flourish, they sanitized the information and put the contents onto a company system... and nobody used it. The line workers had lost ownership; the company had made informal knowledge management into something formal – and killed it.

Information sharing

At the CIA, throughout the inception and implementation of Intellipedia, its founders Dennehy and Burke[115] discovered three core principles of how to best use collaborative tools:

1. Address the broadest audience possible.
2. Think topics, not turf.
3. Replace existing processes with new ones requiring use of the tools.

On the first point, Dennehy said the way the intelligence community and many other organizations work is that employees either have access to a broader, open network or one that's closed and narrow. Intellipedia falls into the former category, which appears to be necessary for good collaboration.

"Start with a base camp of generic information but then also provide a link or a breadcrumb to the more sensitive data that could be in a proprietary database or just a link saying, 'For more information, call John,'" he said.

The second principle is an effort to fight the mentality of ownership. In developing Intellipedia, some agencies wanted to put their name on certain wiki pages and keep other agency names off them. The solution was to add organization credits at the bottom of the page and links to the contributing agencies.

Finally, Dennehy recommends replacing existing processes. "You can throw all these tools out on a network and expect people to jump in there and start using them – but they won't," he said. "People are busy with doing their day-to-day work."

He suggested migrating some of the regular everyday processes to collaboration tools. For example, the content of an email can easily be moved to a blog, discussion page or wiki.

"All of us can agree that we have email overload; when you start moving into these tools, you still get email but they're just notifications you can throw away. All of the rich content you want to preserve is captured in these tools."

Burke says that to successfully implement Web 2.0 technology, companies must let users control the tools. That can be a daunting task for many companies, he noted. "Give up control, and your employees will do you right. Fight for all your life against locked-down, closed spaces. For two years, we have fought against that. Every other call was, 'How do I lock a page?' or, 'How do I create a private page?'"

Some companies are concerned about sharing content. Geoff Weber, a principal at professional audit, tax and advisory services provider KPMG's federal practice says in a Collaboration Tools report, "How do you control what's posted and what information is provided? Yes, wikis allow for quick online knowledge sharing, but the downside is that it allows anyone to post and share."[116] In some cases, they can lead to a consensus of opinion – right or wrong – being seen and disseminated as fact.

For these reasons, organizations must put controls in place before implementing any wiki, he says. To start with, the software should be set up so entries cannot be made anonymously. Insisting that entries can't be made anonymously helps to create a sense of responsibility among users. All content – new entries as well as edits of existing information – should have their authors' details attached.

It might be worth assigning someone to oversee the wiki as its site editor too, he suggests. This person would take a governance role, checking the site to ensure that new entries are correctly categorized, well-written and factually correct.

The site editor could also inform new wiki users of the wiki parameters – what can and can't be included.

"Employees should have an explicit description about what goes into a wiki and what should be left out, and it's always a good idea to include popular and commonly-referenced links and materials," says Weber. Finally, "there should be some incentive to get users inspired and excited about the use of a wiki, even if the only benefit is being able to save time".

Social learning

Let the social learning platform grow organically. "Tend it but don't force it", says Jane Hart, social learning consultant and founder of the Centre for Learning and Performance Technologies.[117]

Use viral marketing techniques to promote the site, suggests Hart: "Don't force it on everyone. Work with groups that are enthusiastic and let them talk about it." Gradually, others will want to join in.

Eric Davidove, a senior executive at Accenture, says moving to a more collaborative learning environment – one where a central training organization, driven by top-down executive inputs, has less control – is a "huge cultural shift for most organizations".[118]

L&D needs to work with senior leadership to conduct a business case analysis of where opportunities exist to improve employee productivity and performance through an improved learning environment. "State those opportunities explicitly in terms of wasted spending as well as opportunities to generate better business results," he recommends.

L&D also needs to evaluate the merits of the available technologies, as well as the business and learning needs those technologies address.

It needs to show proof that social learning can work and it can do that by starting with a workable 'proof of concept', followed by a pilot test involving a representative sample of the employee population. "Test the technology, function, usability, content, learning networks and reward programmes," he suggests.

L&D also needs to monitor the usage, gather feedback and measure the results, and then feed that back into subsequent releases of the social learning solution.

It's well worth the effort, he says. "Social and collaborative environments that leverage informal learning and web 2.0 capabilities can deliver both more efficient and more effective learning with improved impacts on the business.

"Time to competence can be significantly improved in this environment because learning experiences are tailored to employees' needs. Because content is rated and filtered through those who know best – the users – it is more likely to produce successful results."

The US Army may be one of the last places where many would expect to find people using social learning technology, but in fact its online community for commanders has become an important source of learning for officers serving throughout the world.

Majors Nate Allen and Tony Burgess met at West Point, the US Military Academy, in the 1980s. In time, they found themselves commanding army companies in separate battalions (a company usually consists of three or four platoons, equivalent to 100 to 130 soldiers). Living next door to each other on their Hawaii base, they spent many evenings sitting on Allen's front porch, comparing notes while discussing matters ranging from operational training to communication with the spouses of soldiers.

Both found that what they learned from their conversations was having a positive impact on their units and they started looking for ways they could share their experience with others.[119]

Their search eventually led them to the internet and their first action was to publish an online book they had written, called *Taking the Guidon*.[120] The interactive nature of the internet quickly led to conversations being struck between other interested individuals and it was from these conversations that the idea of an online community website was born.

CompanyCommand.com

With the help of a colleague familiar with internet technology and using their own savings, Allen and Burgess launched a website called CompanyCommand. com. Deciding that army commanders were capable of sharing information without compromising security, the site had minimal protection and there was no official endorsement sought from the army command.

The site features 12 sections, ranging from 'Warfighting' to 'Soldiers and Family'. Each section is broken into discussion threads that cover subjects as diverse as mortar attacks and grief counselling.

The site was quickly adopted by the officers in Iraq as one of the main sources of information about fighting a war that was increasingly different from anything their traditional training had prepared them for.

Allen and Burgess set out clear values when they created the CompanyCommand. com site. They wanted to use the internet to recreate the experience of sharing experiences, anecdotes and advice on Allen's porch and to create a community of officers. Key to this was their stated values:

- Positive, with a focus on solutions
- Passion for quality
- Committed to the army
- Innovative and creative
- 'Grass Roots' – generated by the users.

As well as these key values, Allen and Burgess also made several assumptions that helped form the philosophy behind the site:

- The knowledge of the profession resides in the minds of its members
- Connecting leaders allows them to fulfil their professional identity
- Every member has valuable knowledge to share and is intrinsically motivated to do so
- Conversations transform
- We must add best-of-class value to serving company commanders
- Leaders learn best through their experience
- If they build it, they will come... grass roots ownership.

Allen and Burgess took steps to ensure that the site got off to a good start. Before launching it, they set up an informal team, all of whom volunteered without the prospect of remuneration, to run the various different sections of the site. This ensured that any posts that went onto the site received some form of response, with the team often using their own personal networks to get answers to the questions posed. Ultimately, however, the success of the site would be down to the officers that used it. In the event, usage increased dramatically in the first few months following its launch, from 11,000 site hits in February 2000 to 150,000 in August of the same year.

CompanyCommand.com is an example of informal learning in action, offering significant benefits to officers using the site:

- Information that officers find is practical, because it is based on real life experiences and reflections on what went well and what could have been done to make things better
- Advice on the site is also the most up-to-date available – manuals and initial training will eventually become redundant, but the information that is posted by officers on CompanyCommand.com could be as recent as a few minutes old
- Officers get the information they need when they need it – once a thread is posted, there are usually a number of responses within 30 minutes; this is in addition to the information that is already contained within the site
- The site acts as a support network – many aspects of an officer's job can be emotionally, as well as physically, demanding; when dealing with tragic events, having the support and advice of fellow officers can make the job less harrowing and help individuals feel less isolated
- Officers use the site to prepare themselves for command. The front page of the site states that it is for 'Company Commanders – past,

present and future…', and it is being used by junior officers to prepare mentally for what they can expect when they are posted to a war zone, whether it is their first time or a return posting.

One such person, Stan, went to Iraq expecting to be a staff officer throughout his deployment, not a commander. However, when a company commander in his unit was killed in action, Stan was told to prepare to take command immediately. He used CompanyCommand to connect with three experienced commanders who had gone through similar experiences. They were able to advise Stan on how to help the unit deal with the grief of losing their commander as well as how to enable the unit to get back on its feet.[121]

Such was the success and widespread use of the site that the army began to take an interest. In 2002, the site was taken onto the army's secure server and given a protected military address. The army also began to pay the expenses involved in running CompanyCommand and enlisted the four founders of the site to complete PhDs and become professors at West Point, where running the site would be part of their jobs. CompanyCommand.com, and hence informal learning, now form part of the US army's official approach to leadership development.

It shows that people will use these tools if they believe they are owned and managed by the users, not interfered with by the organization, and if they provide genuine benefits to the users. The tools must also be easy to use and access so that there are minimal barriers between the users and the knowledge bank. As I've said throughout this book, the easier a system is to use, and the higher the perceived ownership of the system by the users, the more it will be used.

There is an understandable desire on the part of organizations to control and clean up this kind of user-generated resource and make sure it only has the right messages and so on. Unfortunately, such moves are counter-productive, as they tend to make it look company controlled.

Internal social media platforms

There are a number of new platforms for use inside organizations which offer the characteristics of public social media platforms, such as Facebook, Twitter, Flickr, YouTube and LinkedIn.

An early example of such a system was built in-house by British Telecom (BT), with assistance from external consultants. It is BT's Dare2Share programme, an internal YouTube-style podcasting platform, which allows employees to create, find and view learning segments (podcasts, discussion threads, links, blogs, RSS feeds and other traditional knowledge assets, such as documents, courses and portals links) and also discuss and debate the content being created. Staff can view content online or offline; they can comment on and rate each piece, as well as report inaccurate content. Staff can also contact the authors directly.

The system means learning is immediate, relevant and presented in the context of the work. Learning segments are short and are available on a variety of devices. High-quality content is quickly identified and utilized; experts are easily discovered and contacted, and the learning experience is personalized and social.

The initiative to set up the system came out of research at BT that found its people learnt more from each other than they did through their formal training programmes. BT had been spending about £100 million a year developing and delivering formal training – learning events that the research showed were ineffective and that were, according to employees, too rigid, too generic and too far removed from the realities of their work environment.[122]

Eric Davidove, senior executive at Accenture, which worked with BT to improve the business impact of enterprise learning, says that before the advent of Dare2Share, a large number of the BT workforce had numerous and critical performance needs that were not being met by those formal learning events.

Analysis showed that field engineers were not provided with the opportunity to learn and develop during down time; team leaders independently and unknowingly conducted redundant safety briefings; sales people wasted days trying to find answers, best practices and experts; line managers answered the same questions over and over again, and people spent too much time and money travelling to and from classroom training sessions.

"When we computed the business case – in terms of lost productivity, excess expense and redundant activities – we arrived at a conservative estimate that correcting these situations could save the company at least £8 million per year," he recalls.

"In addition, we compiled data from secondary research about the improved employee productivity and performance that can result from social learning, and from more effectively capturing and reusing tacit knowledge. Clearly it was worth pursuing a better learning environment."

At the time, BT also had a problem with service quality. Repair professionals who had been dispatched to resolve a problem would realize they didn't know how to fix it and would then have to return to their office for help and make a second call. It was a very expensive situation and had a disastrous impact on customer satisfaction.

A large number of the repair people were given a video camera to take to work. Each was asked to video themselves solving various problems in the field and to upload them so others could see the service tricks they'd learned.

Davidove said, "Dare2Share is an extraordinary solution for an extraordinary business need – it offers BT a coherent way to support information creation and sharing, team communication and coordination, professional communities and informal 'social' interactions."

It's an environment that encourages people to experiment, innovate, collaborate, communicate and share their experience and knowledge in engaging ways, he says. "This knowledge sharing has a positive impact on how other employees serve customers, find information or solve problems."

What do employees think? A BT programme director said, "We all use our networks on a day to day basis to get things done. The power of Dare2Share is that it helps you broaden that network and gives you a structure that you can tap into easily."

A BT field engineer said, "There are lots of technical procedures which are dead simple to do, but which people do once in a blue moon, so they've normally lost their book or can't remember how to do it. A podcast of these processes saves so much time and reduces mistakes."

Technology has now enabled a social knowledge management system that would have been impossible to achieve ten years ago.

Another example comes from International Computers Limited (ICL), a UK information technology service provider. Several of its business groups wanted to improve the speed and quality of their services to customers. Elizabeth Lank, ICL's programme director for mobilizing knowledge, used an intranet that gave each of the company's 20 business units its own website.[123]

At first, few employees used it, but then it was modified to support people across those units who were working on similar problems. Thereafter, it was used – in a single year – by more than 300 'communities of practice', including customer teams, project teams, skill-building communities, and temporary special-interest groups, such as the 35 people, in seven countries, developing digital signatures.

Communities of practice are groups of people who share and learn from one another face-to-face and virtually. They're held together by a common interest in a body of knowledge and are driven by a desire and need to share problems, experiences, insights, templates, tools and best practices. The members of such a community deepen their knowledge by interacting on an ongoing basis.

Each ICL community decides when to form, who can join, and what to publish; Lank says she just provides a facility that makes interaction easy. An electronic 'nagging' service, for example, reminds groups when their documents have remained on the server past a predetermined review-by date. Communities "don't need a lot of encouragement to form because it's natural if they're working on an issue together; you just need to encourage them to use technology to support what they're doing," she says.

If you are going to use social media as a platform to facilitate and drive informal learning, you need to consider the fundamentals of the community you wish to create. The questions L&D needs to consider, according to Arthur Chan of Management IQ, include what do staff and employees want from a virtual learning environment; do employees just want a place where they can post questions and get feedback; does the organization value interactivity and the ability to engage in online conversations; do employees prefer online tutorials so they can learn things at their own pace or do they want daily tips, and do they want a single platform where they can get the latest news in their industry?[124]

"By firstly considering why social media should be used in organizational learning, it will help guide which social media platforms L&D departments could invest in," he says. For example, if employees want tutorials for machinery, online videos may be the most appropriate option. If they have problems managing time and want tips, then a micro-blog may be the best solution.

Discussions around the workplace

Of course, social learning and collaboration can easily take place without the social media platforms and investments in technology. Consider the 'water-cooler' conversations. They won't always be about work, but often are. Check where they are happening and provide white boards so ideas can be captured and discussed more easily. Ideas will often flow in such informal settings.

Provide employees with a schedule that allows lunchtime conversations as well as a location for buying or taking good food and a convivial atmosphere (one in which they're likely to meet acquaintances and new people).

Chapter 8

Managing your learnscape

"Live as if you were to die tomorrow. Learn as if you were to live forever."

Mahatma Gandhi

Learning is a skill we all have; however, it is clear that some people are far better at learning than others. Despite the incredible importance of learning in our lives, there is little in the formal education system to teach us how to learn. It is well established that there are different learning styles, yet students at school and university are seldom made aware of this, nor of how they can best learn, given their own style. The subject may be touched on in formal workplace learning, but even then it is often a quick skim over the ideas and perhaps a questionnaire to establish a style or preference.

Learning as a skill seems to be treated with lower priority than skills that can be directly applied to the job. This is in part due to the one-size-fits-all approach of most formal training. There is now a pressing need to move from a strategy based on the delivery of training to one based on support for learning in today's service-led and knowledge-driven economy.

The idea of helping people to learn effectively links with the idea of the learnscape, discussed in chapter 2. The learnscape is the environment in an organization within which people learn. The way that environment is managed has a massive impact on how well people learn and what they learn. As with any complex environment, the people navigating it will need some help and instructions on how to do that effectively.

Ideas and examples

Here are a number of ideas to help you manage the learnscape you are responsible for.

Learning about learning

It is important that people know about learning: how vital it is to them and their job, how ubiquitous it really is, and that much of what they learn is via informal learning. Develop a common understanding throughout the organization of what learning is, so that discussions about learning in the workplace can be meaningful.

In addition to being better informed about the whole concept of learning, it is also very useful if people have an understanding of how they, as individuals, learn best, so they can choose channels of information that suit their own learning style. These choices mean we normally have a small number of resources we use regularly and these consist of our favourite search engine, social networking site, blogs and so on. We all develop our own places to go to find or share information. To a greater or lesser extent, we all develop a personal learning environment, and it is worth teaching people how to do this well.

Personal learning environment (PLE)

The term PLE is used in university and academic circles to describe the tools, communities and services that constitute the individual educational platforms learners use to direct their own learning and pursue educational goals. A PLE is frequently contrasted with a learning management system, in that an LMS tends to be course-centric, whereas a PLE is learner-centric. At the same time, a PLE may or may not intersect with an institutional LMS, and individuals might integrate components of an LMS into the educational environments that they construct for themselves.

A typical PLE, for example, might incorporate blogs, where students comment on what they are learning, and their posts may reflect information drawn from across the web — on sites like YouTube or in RSS feeds from news agencies. While most discussions of PLEs focus on online environments, the term encompasses the entire set of resources that a learner uses to answer questions, provide context and illustrate processes. The term refers, not to a specific service or application, but rather to an idea of how individuals approach the task of learning.

Part of the management of a learnscape is in ensuring that people can build and access their PLEs easily.

Information gathering

One of the key skills required for effective informal learning in our technical age is finding information online. Everybody on the internet uses search engines, and yet very few have learned to do more than just type in a few words and click 'Search'. There is a rich functionality in all the major search engines that is largely untapped. Promote the use of better searching skills through coaching, e-learning modules or job aids.

Circulate helpful URLs, especially with testimonials from colleagues who have recently used one. If someone in sales has found a great source of time management tips, there's a very good chance that other people in the organization will find it useful too. Encourage employees to share useful links they find while doing their work.

Help employees to assess the value and veracity of the information they find. The ability to discern good information from poor is a vital skill in today's world of information glut, where a lot of what is published online is poor or unproven.

Incorporate internet and information gathering skills into formal training courses and ensure that any resources provided by the organization are well sign-posted to users.

One area that is often overlooked by people is the online help available within the applications they use every day. Encourage people to use online help before they call technical support. If they do call the internal help desk, ensure that part of the resolution involves showing the user where they could have found the answer for themselves.

It's important that help desks are capable of assisting with current problems and issues. Employees will shun help desks if they find they're unable to provide updated assistance. Worse, they'll spread the word that the help desk is actually incapable of providing relevant assistance.

To encourage employees to use a help desk, publicize help desk success stories via the company intranet, in-house newsletters or e-zines and so on. Give help desk personnel tasks that bring them into contact with people throughout the organization. Also consider establishing help desks for functions other than computer tech support.

Another opportunity for information gathering occurs when people are interacting with others outside the organization. Commonly, this would be suppliers and customers, but it also includes professional groups and membership organizations.

Help defray expenses, such as membership fees and travel to regional and national meetings. Encourage professional group members to report on their group's activities to others in your organization, through informal lunchtime presentations, brief articles in department emails or newsletters, and posts on the company or departmental blog or on a company forum.

Establish subject matter experts

Subject matter experts are the natural hubs of information. They are the 'go to' people who will always have an answer, or know where to get it. And their time is very valuable. They are valuable when doing their own work, and valuable when assisting others to do their work more effectively.

Some of these information mavens will be good at helping other people who are less experienced; some will not be any good at all. Some will delight in doing it; some won't. Pick your people carefully and offer them assistance in becoming better mentors and coaches. That might mean coaching them or having them attend a course on the basics of coaching. There is better value in the long term if they adopt a coaching approach.

Of course, some subject matter experts won't want to share their expertise. They might think the more knowledge they have, the more valued they will be. "The more I control what I know, the more indispensable I will be and my job is safe."

Some subject matter experts are so engaged and wrapped up with what they do that they really don't feel they have the time to help others. Perhaps they really don't want to be bothered. So you have to find the ones who want to share the information they have. You might have to help them learn how to share information effectively. They need to be able to help learning take place, rather than just transfer knowledge. You also need to reduce that person's other responsibilities, so they have time to coach others and to make it part of their official duties.

You also need to provide them with channels (wikis, blogs, space in the corporate magazine or newsletter and so on) to make information available.

There are all sorts of things you can do to enable them to have a visibility and a voice. And that visibility and voice might be the reward that they want for doing it. Who knows what will motivate them to participate in knowledge sharing? The way to find out is to ask.

You could send them to conferences to get information and then rework it to suit whatever the company needs internally. That might be something they have not done before and could be highly valued by them.

Encourage them to fetch information from their own sources, and then push it internally. Ensure they are monitoring what's going on in the informal networks within the organization, because they are your gatekeeper for bad information. They're the people who will be able to stop bad information going viral in your informal networks, because they'll notice it happening and they'll be able to say, "Wait a minute. That's not right. Here's the real answer."

Development of informal coaches and mentors

There will always be people who will help those new to the organization. This is not usually a formal role; it is just in their nature to want to help others. These people may or may not be your local subject matter experts.

Provide easy-to-use resources for those who act as informal coaches or mentors, and for the people they are assisting. Help them to help people learn and build up more self-sufficiency by pointing people to relevant and useful resources so they know where to go next time.

You can take a step beyond informal coaching and consider providing a formal peer coaching system, in which a coaching coordinator schedules peer coaching sessions, arranges for work substitutes, if necessary, and coaches the coaches.

Another aspect of mentoring is job observation and shadowing. Appoint a coordinator to schedule and manage these relationships, and make sure participants know how to make the most of their time together. Ask shadows and experts to report on their experiences in staff meetings, newsletters, on the intranet and in-house social network.

Provide public recognition to experts for their part in helping shadows get up to speed.

In addition to the one-to-one mentoring model, you can also put novices in a team where they can learn from others more experienced than them. Ensure that both experts and novices understand their additional roles and responsibilities to make teaming work.

Experts may not be skilled at teaching, so make sure they know they may need to slow down. Encourage them to put themselves in the novice's place so they understand their challenges and needs. Encourage them to reflect on why they do things in a certain way. Very often, experts have reached a stage of unconscious competence which makes it difficult for them to articulate how they do what they do.

Encourage novices to observe consciously, to elicit knowledge from the experts, and be willing to speak out when they don't understand something.

Informal learning during training

Build in opportunities for informal learning to take place when you plan any kind of formal training. Instead of trying to keep people busy in between formal learning sessions, let them find their own learning space. Consider how you can add in social and discussion time during and after the course, so people share and build on the ideas they are learning during the formal parts of the training.

As an adjunct to formal training, or used in a more informal on-demand way, many organizations have invested in libraries of e-learning modules. Find different ways of publicizing the individualized instruction materials that are available in-house. In addition, some employees may seek online learning that is not available in-house, so provide support to individuals who want to buy or rent materials or subscribe to online materials.

Recognize and give credit to individuals who have completed individualized instruction in performance reviews or in public forums.

Cross teams

Cross-functional teams are typically composed of individuals who have a functional home base (for example, engineering, personnel, marketing and so on), but who work collaboratively on issues or processes requiring diverse resources.

There are four key areas that distinguish cross-functional teamwork from more conventional teams, according to a study carried out by the Institute of Employment Studies in 2000:[125]

1. Functional diversity.
2. Competing identities.
3. Integration into the organizational structure.
4. Performance expectation.

The members of a cross-functional team seldom have an explicit expectation of what they might learn, nor are they always conscious of what they have learnt. Measuring both learning methods and outcomes is therefore difficult.

The IES study illustrates how team members learn via four particular routes:

1. Direct transfer of knowledge or skills from other experts.
2. Picking things up from observing others in action.
3. Collective problem-solving and experimentation.
4. Consolidating prior experience and reframing new insights.

A critical success factor in team learning is having an appropriate mix of expertise in the team (it is, of course, equally important that individual experts are prepared and able to share and otherwise impart their knowledge).

The study's co-authors, Kettley and Hirsh, say the cross-functional team experience is a powerful opportunity for self-development, even for those employees who join with little or no learning intent.

There are at least three definable categories or types of learning distinguishable from one another in terms of the knowledge and skills acquired by cross-functional team members:

1. Learning about self – for example, enhanced personal effectiveness via generic interpersonal, interactive and communication competencies, such as influencing others, handling conflict, listening and feedback
2. Learning about the organization – for example, a better understanding of the interdependencies of different parts of the organization and related processes (systems thinking); appreciation of the complexity of managing change and its implications for problem-solving and decision making; skills in identifying improvement opportunities and building a shared vision; collaborative enquiry, clarifying (internal and external) customer requirements and so on
3. Learning about other specialisms – for example, the acquisition or appreciation of particular functional or job competencies, and tools and techniques typically used by other specialisms/functions. Individuals become familiar with the requirements of others, their working methods, professional standards, regulatory requirements and so on.

The team members interviewed in the report consistently reported that it was the softer skills around their self-awareness and personal effectiveness that they had developed most. This was borne out by their responses to the survey, with 40 per cent ranking learning about self.

Below are some of the key contextual factors that directly impact upon the learning of a cross-functional team:

• Explicit consideration should be given to learning, for the individual and the organization, before, during and after the team-experience. This includes a positive attitude on the part of an individual member's home function and monitoring the level of interaction across boundaries with the rest of the organization. For example, employers will limit the potential of valuable learning if they impose arbitrary deadlines upon the team, and/or evaluate team and individual effectiveness by ill-considered performance measures.

- Diversity within the team and autonomy to organize the work of the team – team members should not be appointed and allocated responsibilities solely on the basis of their functional expertise.
- The degree of close working and interaction – cross-functional teams benefit enormously from being co-located. Equally important is continuity and consistency of membership. It may seem a good idea to bring in new blood now and again to refresh the team effort, but this can undermine the team dynamic and levels of trust essential to team learning.
- Team processes should be used for learning and honest discussion of difficulties.

Job sharing

Another way to provide employees with learning opportunities is to offer them job swaps and, if it is necessary to enable them to do a different job, you could also offer formal training courses, e-learning courses and so on. Job sharing provides employees with the opportunity to work flexibly and to learn from another colleague.

Switch people between departments so they can learn how other departments function. It can be very enlightening for someone in logistics, for example, to spend some time in manufacturing and to realize how important logistics are if the organization is to get the right component to the production line at the right time. Likewise, it can be very enlightening for someone from the manufacturing floor to spend some time on trucks and logistics to discover that it's not so easy getting the right materials to the right place at the right time.

When people take part in job swaps or start a new job, have them keep an 'astonishment log' during their first few weeks. What do they see that astonishes them? It might be something the new office or department does well or poorly, in their opinion, or that they see what is not being done, but which should be. If anything happens that astonishes them, they write it down. In other words, "You're doing that. Why?" Or "I can't believe you're not doing it this way". Or "How can you get away with that over here? We can't do that over in our department".

They should record anything that astonishes them, from good or bad management or good or bad processes and systems, through to inaccurate information or things they wished they had known where they used to work.

It's important to capture people's first impressions in the job because, after about a month, they will have become accustomed to what happens and won't see it as noteworthy. It's like getting used to a smell in a room.

The 'astonishment log' is a practical tool that can be used to capture learning and make it more readily available. Just be aware that if it's not real and honest, it's going to have less value. This honesty can of course have repercussions if the log contains comments that do not reflect well on the person's temporary line manager or senior managers. Some care must be taken with who sees the log and how it is used. The level of care required is an indication of the openness of the culture and of the individuals concerned with feedback and learning opportunities.

Internal and external information sources

Learnscape information also comes from internal company magazines, where someone within the organization writes an article about a success or best practice, for example, and it then gets promoted and read by employees. Internal sources also include procedure and process manuals and employee handbooks, crib sheets, working practice guides and so on. The range of possible internal sources for information to flow into a learnscape are really only limited by the imagination.

It could be a library of books, manuals or industry magazines that are located where people have lunch and coffee breaks. It could be magazines that are peripheral to your industry, and the annual reports of competitors and other industry information.

It could be online libraries that contain information your employees will find relevant. There are general e-books or articles on things like management and more specific ones on things such as auditing rules, food hygiene or construction safety. Some are free; some are subscription services. Of course, you have to consider the barriers that might stop someone from using the information.

You can subscribe to an online resource that's got wonderful information, but if it's difficult to navigate, people aren't going to use it.

What can be really beneficial is if one of your subject matter experts has something published in a trade journal. And then people see it in the trade journal and say, "Oh, wow, look. John's famous. Look. He's got his photograph in this trade journal." So if you can get some of your subject matter experts to contribute articles that other people in the organization will then see, there's a whole credibility lift on that, particularly if it's a printed trade magazine. It gives your subject matter expert kudos, both internally and externally.

I have a personal story which relates to this. Years ago, I was working as a consultant for a manufacturing company. The company had held prime place in its industry for many years. Unfortunately, that had led to complacency to such an extent that quality control had begun to slip. Worse, a couple of overseas companies had started to move into the same market. The company's senior management knew this – they could see sales dropping off and they were struggling to maintain market share – but they couldn't seem to communicate that they needed to improve the quality of their output to the people on the shop floor.

They asked me, "How can we get our people to be aware that we're now in a competitive situation? Some of our long-term employees have never known what that's like." I suggested they put some of their competitors' annual reports in the tearoom. They were taken aback, but did what I suggested.

Within two weeks, people on the shop floor were talking about the competitors. This obviously got the message through, because over the next few months, the quality of the output began to improve. They then took things a stage further and purchased some of the competing products and left them in the tea room for people to dismantle and examine.

That's an informal learning intervention. It was very low key and low cost. At the time, I must confess that I had no idea whether or not it would work, but considered that anything was worth a try. Fortunately, it worked.

An often underutilized information source is external consultants. If they are brought into your organization, make sure that part of their remit is skills transfer. Ensure that some of what they know is left behind after they have finished their contract.

Self-generated information

This comes in two forms. One is trial and error. You know what good looks like, and you can see the gap between your current results and what you would like them to be. You seek to close the gap by trying different methods and noticing whether the gap grows or shrinks.

In a work situation, trial and error is a double edged sword. It can lead to new and valuable information, and it can also be a costly exercise. L&D can play a role in helping people use trial and error responsibly by including it in their initiatives to help people learn how to learn.

The second is when we derive new information from what we already know. We can mull over ideas and create new ones by combining information and using our imagination. We can conduct thought experiments and come to conclusions. We often then proceed to testing them in some way to gather yet more information to support our deductions.

Another often undervalued source of information that leads to learning is that gained through observation of colleagues. This can be purposeful observation where the outcome is to learn about what they are doing, but it is often unconscious observation that has the larger effect. We tend to mimic those around us who are good at what they do. If you think about it, this is a natural survival characteristic that has been part of our makeup, probably for millions of years. In fact, it is almost impossible not to mimic those around us. We copy gestures and accents, we copy the way people conduct a business meeting or negotiate, we copy the way they hold a tool of the trade, and we copy the way people dress in order to fit in.

Wherever we are in whatever occupation we are in, there is a flood of information that we receive and unconsciously align with. Sometimes this alignment is dormant until an event triggers it. An example would be when someone gets promoted to a management role and starts acting the way they have seen other managers act in the past.

Barriers to information

People will only ever learn inside a learnscape when it provides new information. If there's no new information, there's no learning to be had.

If people need information, which is one of the key 'fertilizers' for a learnscape, then making it readily available makes sense. The easier it is to get at needed information, the less motivation or tenacity is required from the person wanting the information.

The opposite is also true. The harder the information is to get at, the more time and energy employees must invest to get it, which means they might just give up. In this case, what they learn (because they are always learning) is how to get by without the needed information, and how to make sure they don't get blamed for the resulting mess.

You can exert good influence on your learnscape by lowering the barriers between workers and the information they require.

This is where it becomes of paramount importance that managers are involved with the learnscape. As an L&D person, you will have to involve managers, because so many of these things are managerial and not L&D decisions. The managers need to be invested in the learnscape too. Think of L&D as the head gardener and the managers as gardening assistants, with responsibilities for specific areas of the garden.

Chapter 9

Obstacles you may face

"The knowledge that we consider knowledge proves itself in action. What we now mean by knowledge is information in action, information focused on results."

Peter Drucker

Although many organizational leaders say their employees are their most valuable assets, they often contradict this in practice by neglecting their employees' learning or by allowing barriers to learning, especially informal learning, to remain in their organization.

A barrier to workplace learning and performance can be "any expressed behaviour, attitude, value or action that distracts, impedes or prevents individuals, teams or organizational learning and performance".[126]

Perhaps they are unaware of those barriers, don't have the capacity to overcome them, or don't see the value of investing in the resources required to develop their people.

When obstacles to learning and performance are present, they negatively impact productivity and hinder overall organizational success. When employers remove barriers to performance, progress and positive development occur for individuals and organizations. On the other hand, forcing employees to learn by threatening them with dire consequences can foster a sense of distrust and fear, which effectively paralyzes learning within an organization.

Organizational Development expert Edgar H. Stein says learning something invariably creates one of two kinds of anxiety – learning anxiety, which is the fear of learning something and it being too difficult, and survival anxiety, which is the horrible realization that in order to make it, you're going to have to change.[127]

Survival anxiety is what prisoners of war experience. It's also what organizations use too much of to force learning to take place.

"To the extent that our present managerial practices emphasize the stick over the carrot, companies are building in strong resistance to learning. That's very predictable, because in most organizations managers bully their followers to learn – or else. Then, when the latest corporate change programme turns out to be just another case of the manager crying wolf, and he gets fired as a result, employees settle into a wait-and-see attitude.

"If leaders really want workers to learn new things, they have to educate them about economic realities in a way that makes their messages credible. When management gains that credibility, it can create the kind of anxiety that leads to a safe learning environment. In this respect, it's important to distinguish between forcing people to learn something they can see the need to accept – such as new computer skills – and asking them to learn something that seems questionable to them. There will always be learning anxiety, but if the employee accepts the need to learn, then the process can be greatly facilitated by good training, coaching, group support, feedback, positive incentives, and so on."

Learning is not always welcomed throughout an organization. Stein points out that when small groups begin to learn and innovate, they can make others within the company anxious and envious.

"Learning most often begins with a small group and only gradually spreads across the organization and then up. In fact, it's rather common for individuals or small groups to make major strides in their own learning before the rest of the organization does. When those learners begin to innovate, however, they make other people anxious and envious, so the organization's autoimmune system rejects them. Indeed, individual learning can be a dangerous thing when the organization's value system and culture don't have enough freedom to allow individuals to do what they need to do."

So how can innovative informal learners protect themselves from a cultural backlash?

"Resilience is often the ability to make yourself invisible. In organizations, individual learners lie, cheat, go underground– they do whatever they have to do to remain invisible. And in large organizations, going underground isn't that difficult.

"There is this wonderful story about the guy who was first proposing the Personal Computer project to IBM's senior management. He had to get the board's approval for his project and was given only five minutes on the agenda at the end of the day

"He was unhappy about this until his boss told him how lucky he was: 'Because you only have those few minutes, they are going to hear whatever they want to hear, and your project will go through.' The implication is that IBM might never have approved the project if senior managers had given the learners in the organization careful consideration."

There are some common causes of resistance (often expressed as disinterest) that L&D may anticipate or encounter, when transitioning from formal to informal learning.

In the case of stakeholders, resistance tends to be rooted in the following two areas:

1. Concern about the perceived loss of authority or control: informal learning that incorporates social elements – commenting, contributing and crowd sourcing – can cause concerns about the 'right' information being shared. This is understandable, as it's a shift from formal learning, where the content goes through an approval process before it's disseminated, and then usually isn't revised until the next official update.
2. Concern that informal learning will not be effective: consider that measurement of formal learning – course registrations, assessment scores and learner reaction scores – won't translate precisely to

informal learning. Informal learning can provide meaningful metrics and analytics, but what's measured and communicated will be different.

For learners, anxiety arises from other two other main sources:

1. No role models for engagement: though learners may not articulate this concern, informal learning is a shift and they may not know what the right behaviour is, so they wonder "Should I comment? Should I contribute? Am I expert enough? How much is too much?"
2. Belief that informal learning will not be relevant or helpful to their work: learners today have access to many sources of information, so they may see informal learning as another drag on their information load, rather than something beneficial.

When Intellipedia was being launched by the CIA, it was middle managers who resisted the spy agency's effort to provide Web 2.0 tools to internal employees.

"Middle management is about making the trains run on time," says Don Burke, one of the co-founders of Intellipedia. "Their job is to do today's job. Change is extraordinarily disruptive. The incentives in our hierarchy are not designed to leverage these kinds of fundamental changes. The incentives are designed to reward the people who are making the trains run on time."

It's important to know the barriers employees might have to learning.

Adult learners have their own personal view of the world and what is needed to survive and succeed in their personal endeavours; they even have their own personal view of success.

Their views are formed from internal and external influences, in both their past and present experience. These views in turn form their motivation and barriers to learning.

Understanding which are the intrinsic and extrinsic factors affecting motivation and understanding the barriers to learning, enables L&D and managers to focus their efforts on the root cause of any resistance. It further allows the facilitators of learning to get a better understanding of learners and find ways to motivate them and remove any barriers to learning.

After all, even though your organization may have an outstanding learning environment, if people can't get over these barriers and access the learning environment, they won't learn.

Blocks and barriers

Below are some of the more common blocks and barriers that you may need to tackle.

Negative experiences of learning

Many people had negative experiences during their schooldays which still influence their perceptions of what learning involves. They see learning as something that only happens properly in a classroom setting. They may, in addition, associate learning with failure, which can lead to a lack of self-esteem.

People may doubt their ability to learn, given their experiences in the school system. They may have been called 'stupid' as children, and taken that as a truth. They may even believe that nothing they do really matters.

Many people need re-educating about learning and how it pervades their everyday lives, so they can embrace it rather than see it as something to avoid.

Lack of direction

Without leadership and engagement, people are unlikely to have a clear idea of what they want to achieve in their work. They will lack the impetus to move forward or to stretch towards that goal, and so to learn what they need to learn to reach the goal.

Without the desire to learn, people will often do the minimum of tasks required, without processing or understanding the information, and they may not even try at all.

However, an interesting thing happens when people are clear about their goal; their Reticular Activating System (RAS) will kick in. It's an area within the human brain that regulates cardiovascular, respiratory and motor responses and receives input from the senses via the central nervous system. It then 'filters' those inputs, only allowing through information that has some importance to the individual. Through these functions, it controls a person's ability to pay attention and to be awake or asleep, and it allows them to be aware of activities that are happening in their environment.

The RAS is the brain's equivalent of a Google Alert. It decides what is and is not important to the individual and what he or she needs to pay attention to. The 'filter' sits between the subconscious and conscious minds, and is programmed by the conscious mind. It is this ability to programme the filter that makes the Reticular Activating System so important in achieving goals.

When an important piece of information is received by the individual's sensory system, the RAS brings that piece of information to his or her attention.

The RAS is unable to distinguish between real or synthetic events and stimuli; it believes the messages it receives. Therefore it is possible to programme it by creating specific goals in the imagination; the more sensory specific the better. The 'filter' then raises the individual's awareness to items that can help in achieving that goal. If an individual thinks, talks, reviews and writes about a specific goal, the RAS filter is reinforced to select information about that goal.

It is clear from this that having a goal, and the subsequent activation of the RAS, is a critical part of the process of learning informally.

Stress

Stress is a major block to learning simply because, when the body is overtaxed, the chemical overload shuts down short-term memory, recall, physical growth, sex drive and much more. This affects people's ability to learn (as well as their emotional and physical wellbeing). When people are highly stressed, they tend to work on automatic pilot. The goal is to escape the stressful situation, and learning is one of the furthest things from the mind of a highly stressed worker.

One of the causes of stress in today's workplace is the very transient and short nature of all the tasks that people are engaged in. They hardly get started on something before they are whisked away onto something else – a phone call, an email, or an enquiry from a colleague. After each interruption, it takes people a significant period to re-establish connection with the task from which they were distracted.

Anxiety about the results/impact of learning

Stein said anxiety inhibits learning, but it is also necessary if learning is going to happen at all.[128]

"To understand this, we're going to have to speak about something managers don't like to discuss – the anxiety involved in motivating people to 'unlearn' what they know and learn something new."

People are afraid of trying something new in case it is too difficult and they will look stupid in the attempt or they will have to part from old habits that have worked in the past.

"Learning something new can cast us as the deviant in the groups we belong to. It can threaten our self-esteem and, in extreme cases, even our identity," Stein says.

"People can't be talked out of their learning anxieties; they're the basis for resistance to change. Given the intensity of those fears, people would never try something new unless they experienced the second form of anxiety, survival anxiety.

"Like prisoners of war, potential learners experience so much hopelessness through survival anxiety that eventually they become open to the possibility of learning."

Lack of time, money or space

These barriers apply to the more formal end of the learning spectrum, where the learning that is taking place is not integrated within the work activity.

The amount of work an employee has to complete may leave little time for learning. Personal commitments may also mean the learner has little time or energy to invest in learning activities.

Usually, a lack of money has more impact on learning endeavours that are not work related (for example, if the individual learner can't afford to pay for evening classes and so on). In the current climate, however, a lack of funding within the workplace will have a direct impact on learning. For example, employees may want to join a professional networking organization, but be unable to do so because the organization simply can't afford the subscription fees.

Another barrier to learning occurs where an individual's workplace or home environment is not conducive to learning (there's no quiet space in which to think or study or they may be on the road for most of their working day, for example).

A culture of fear

Chances are, when people are doing something with new information, they will make mistakes. That's part of the territory. But if a blame culture or 'head on a plate' culture exists, people will avoid trying anything new in case they make a mistake.

Employees have to feel safe if they make a mistake and be able to admit making it when it happens. If they are wary of putting new information into use because they might make a mistake, that's a barrier to using it.

If this is the case, it's up to the manager to delegate things in such a way that those mistakes are acceptable. If they're not acceptable for that activity, the manager needs to delegate in a different way, which means the job will be done by someone more skilled; perhaps shadowed by someone who has not done it before.

The way that people delegate needs to allow people to have new experiences where mistakes can be permitted. Managers need to encourage their direct reports to learn from a mistake, changing what they do so that it is less likely to happen again.

There is a famous story about the founder of IBM, Thomas J. Watson Sr and a young vice president who had spent $10 million on a research project that completely failed. The young man walked into Watson Sr.'s office, apologized for the mistake and offered his resignation.

"You don't have to fire me," he said, "I'll go peacefully. I know I've made a mistake." Watson Sr replied, "Fire you? Why would I fire you? I've just spent $10 million on your education. Now, let's talk about your next assignment."

That is a rather expensive informal learning experience.

Mistakes need to be used as the basis of a lesson. More importantly, the lesson needs to be shared within the organization so that others can also learn. That will only happen in an organization where fear doesn't stalk the corridors.

Little value placed on learning

If an organization doesn't regard learning as a priority, learners may find it difficult to get the support and resources they need to learn. The attitudes of managers and senior executives in such an organization are likely to be neutral or even negative towards learning.

The attitude towards learning is a fundamental characteristic of any learnscape. If the learnscape is not 'learning friendly', then this is one of the first things that needs to be addressed at the most senior level.

The lack of accreditation and application of learning outcomes

One of the motivations to learn is acknowledgement from others (in terms of praise from a superior or a recognized certificate of achievement). If those are not available or too difficult to obtain, people may lack the incentive to try. Similarly, if people don't have the opportunity to transfer what they've learnt into some aspect of their job, they will quickly forget it and be less inclined to bother to learn in the future.

By nature, people usually want more; denying any opportunities for improvement and stretching will dull this desire for growth and the need for learning that goes with it.

The society places no value on learning

If learners live in a society (or in a family) in which little or no value is placed on learning, it is less likely they will be motivated to want to learn or to demonstrate with their behaviours that they have learned.

I had first-hand experience of this as a student in a summertime job where most of the workers were from a particular ethnic group that did not greatly value education. In conversations at work, the elders encouraged me in pursuit of my studies, but clearly did not give similar encouragement to their own families. Their aspirations for their children did not include education, even though they clearly recognised its value for others. This was many years ago and, thankfully, this attitude is changing.

Societal values relating to learning will surface in your learnscape, so you need to be aware of them, as they may set expectations which fall well short of what you desire to achieve.

For individuals involved in informal learning, continuing participation can be threatened by the costs (both time and money), and by peer and family pressures.

Removing blocks and barriers

Force Field Analysis, created by social psychologist Kurt Lewin, is a method for listing, discussing, and assessing the various forces for and against a proposed change. Force Field Analysis is very useful when you want to identify and overcome resistance to change within your organization.

The forces that help you to achieve the change are called 'driving forces' and the forces that resist change are called 'restraining forces'.

Before change, the force field is in equilibrium between forces favourable to change and those resisting it. For change to happen, the status quo must be upset – either by adding conditions favourable to the change or by reducing resisting forces.

Once you've identified the forces, you can develop strategies to reduce the impact of the opposing forces and strengthen the supporting forces.

You can use Force Field Analysis to:

- Determine if a proposed change will get support
- Identify obstacles to successful solutions
- Suggest actions to reduce the strength of the obstacles.

Some forces to consider:

- Available resources
- Traditions

- Vested interests
- Organizational structures
- Relationships
- Social or organizational trends
- Attitudes of people
- Culture
- Regulations
- Personal or group needs
- Present or past practices
- Institutional policies or norms
- Procedures
- Agencies
- Values
- Desires
- Costs
- People
- Events.

Quite often, change doesn't take place because people or systems get in the way. With Force Field Analysis, you can also identify the people, issues or systems that may resist or block change. After analysing the situation and identifying the problems that may occur, you can then work out how to remove the barriers to change.

Force Field Analysis can be used to:

- Investigate the balance of power in an issue
- Identify the most important people (stakeholders) and groups involved or affected
- Identify opponents and allies
- Identify how to influence the target group through action planning.

How to use it:

- Describe the current situation and the desired situation as the vision for the future
- Identify what will happen if no action is taken
- List all the driving and restraining forces for the change
- Allocate a score to each force (using a numerical scale where one is very weak and ten is very strong)

- List, in order of strength, the driving forces on the left and the restraining forces on the right
- Explore the restraining forces and the best way to address them
- Explore the driving forces and the best way of advancing them
- Identify priorities and produce an action plan.

Once you have carried out an analysis, you can decide whether the project or change is viable. If the project has to be delivered to meet a target, the results of the Force Field Analysis can help you to work out how to improve the likelihood of success. At that point, you have some choices:

1. Reduce the strength of the forces opposing a project.
2. Increase the forces pushing a project.
3. Doing both.

Sometimes it's easier to reduce the impact of restraining forces than it is to strengthen driving forces. Once you've identified the factors that may help or hinder your project or planned changes, you can use this knowledge to drive the project. Focus on those things that you can influence.

Bridging the knowing-doing gap

There is often a big gap between knowledge of something and translating that knowledge into action. This is the classic 'knowing-doing gap'. People read something or attend training sessions and resolve to change their behaviour, but quite often there is little action and they lapse into their old behaviours. This relapse is often caused by time pressures, peer pressure, anxiety over one's capabilities and, sometimes, by joyful circumstances (such as feelings that things are going well).

All too often, education and training produce very little change in what managers and organizations actually do. Authors of the *The Knowing-Doing Gap*, Jeffrey Pfeffer and Robert I. Sutton, call this the 'knowing-doing' problem, in which companies fail to take the vital step of transforming knowledge and learning into action.[129]

They explain that one of the main reasons that knowledge management efforts are often divorced from day-to-day activities is that those who design and build the systems have limited knowledge of how people actually use knowledge in their jobs.

"Knowledge management systems rarely reflect the fact that essential knowledge, including technical knowledge, is often transferred between people by stories, gossip and by watching one another work," they say.

"Formal systems can't store knowledge that isn't easily described or codified but is nonetheless essential for doing the work, called tacit knowledge," they say. "So while firms keep investing millions of dollars to set up knowledge management groups, most of the knowledge that is actually used and useful is transferred by the stories people tell to each other, by the trials and errors that occur as people develop knowledge and skill, by inexperienced people watching those more experienced and by experienced people providing close and constant coaching to newcomers."

In other words, most of the knowledge that is useful and used is circulated by informal methods. This means that the knowing-doing gap exists partly because firms misconstrue what their people should know or be seen to know.

The gap between knowing and doing is more important than the gap between ignorance and knowing, according to Pfeffer and Sutton.

The following obstacles prevent many organizations from closing the knowing-doing gap.

1. Talking instead of taking action

One of the biggest barriers to turning knowledge into action is the tendency for people to equate talking about something with actually doing something about it. There is often an unspoken but powerful belief that once a decision has been made to do something, nothing more needs to be done to ensure it is implemented.

Talk is valued because the quantity and quality of it can be assessed instantly, but the quality of leadership or management capability can only be assessed after a greater time lag, when the results are apparent.

In an effort to impress others, people like to use complex language, analysis, ideas and even sentence structures. This too gets in the way of learning. Organizations that are better at learning and translating knowledge into action understand the virtue of simple language, structures and concepts, as well as the power of common sense.

"Simple talk is valuable because it is more likely to lead to action," according to Pfeffer and Sutton. "It is difficult to dispute simple, direct ideas. One may disagree with a simple idea or a simple philosophy, but it is transparent at the outset." Blame and second guessing are less likely when ideas or philosophies are simple.

2. Using the past as a guide for the present and future

People often do what has always been done without reflecting on the effectiveness of their actions. When they confront a new problem, they often look to what has been done in the past and base their actions on that.

To avoid relying on the past as a guide to action, organizations can take one of three actions:

1. Start a new organization or unit which does not inherit the old ways.
2. Make people aware of the problems with doing things in old ways or make it difficult for them to use the old ways.
3. Create and implement new ways of doing things.

3. Fear

If people are afraid for their jobs, their futures, or even for their self-esteem, it is unlikely that they will feel secure enough to do anything but what they have done in the past. Fear will cause them to repeat past mistakes and avoid trying out better ways of doing the work.

People who fear their managers will probably hide bad news from them; they may even lie about what's happening. Fear can lead to falsification of information and the inability to learn.

4. Measurement obstructs good judgment

People focus their attention on what gets measured and tend to ignore anything that is not measured. After all, what is measured is presumed to be important and what is measured gets done.

Unfortunately, the majority of organizations don't measure elements of management practice, business strategy or culture that matter for long-term performance. Instead, they focus on short-term results.

There are often too many end-of-process measures and not enough in-process indicators to help people understand what is currently going right and what is going wrong. End-of-process measures cause those subjected to them to feel a great deal of pressure. The problem is that they are not being measured or controlled on the things that really matter and things that they can directly affect – their specific current behaviours and actions on the job.

Effective measurement systems that will drive behaviour need to be simple enough to focus attention on key elements and fair enough so that people believe they can affect the measures, according to Pfeffer and Sutton. If measures are too powerful in directing people, important elements of behaviour and performance receive too little or no attention, because of the unrelenting emphasis just on the quantitative measures incorporated in the system.

Organizations which are successful at turning knowledge into action measure things that are core to their culture and values and are tied to their basic business model and strategy; they then use these measures to make business processes visible to all employees.

5.   Internal competition

Excessive internal competition can destroy organizations. When internal competition is rife, very little internal learning takes place because people are too busy vying for status and management attention.

Competition can cause people to perceive more distinctions between departments than actually exist and to spend time thinking and talking about those minor, or even imagined, differences. It also makes it more likely that ideas from other departments in the organization will be rejected because they are inconsistent with the group or department's social identity.

Competition inhibits learning and creativity. People focus, not on the task at hand, but instead on what their competitors are doing, on how well they are performing in comparison, and on the reactions of others, such as leaders and peers. Internal competition is especially destructive when people are given complex or difficult tasks that require them to seek help and share ideas with others.

How to turn knowledge into action

The knowing-doing gap can be minimized by dealing with the following factors…

Finding out why before how

Too often, managers want to learn 'how' in terms of detailed practices, behaviours and techniques, rather than 'why' in terms of philosophy and general guidance for action.

Knowing comes from doing and teaching others how

Learning is best done by trying many things, learning from what works and what does not, thinking about what was learned (reflecting), and trying again. And we have all heard the old adage, "the best way to learn something is to teach it."

Action is more important than elegant plans and concepts

Without taking some action, learning is more difficult and less efficient, because it is not grounded in real experience. One slogan to represent this is "Done is better than perfect". This helps to establish a cultural tone that talk and analysis without action are unacceptable.

Failure is an acceptable part of learning

All learning involves some failure, which should be seen as something from which people can continue to learn. To build an action culture, it's critical that it's understood by everyone involved that mistakes will happen. Failure should never be received with anger or negative repercussions.

Fear causes knowing-doing gaps, so drive out fear

Fear in organizations causes many problems. People will not try something new if the outcome is likely to be a career disaster.

Organizations that are successful in turning knowledge and learning into action have leaders who inspire respect and affection, but not fear.

Use cooperation not competition within the organization

Competition within organizations is often regarded as a superior way of managing people, but it has negative consequences. In collaborative, cooperative organizations, people know that the result is the product of common effort, the goal is shared and members' successes are interlinked. This fits perfectly with the whole concept of sharing and collaborating within the context of informal learning.

Measure what matters and what can help turn knowledge into action

Most information systems can show what has happened – but they seldom provide information that is helpful in determining why results have been as they have or what is going to happen in the near future. Organizations need to use in-process measures, as well as outcomes. It's also much better to have a few measures that are directly related to the basic business model, rather than a huge range of measures that produce a lack of focus, with confusion about what is important and what is not.

What leaders do, matters

Leaders of companies that have minimized the knowing-doing gap understand that their most important task is not necessarily to make strategic decisions, but to help build systems that facilitate transformation of knowledge and learning into action in a smooth, reliable way.

Make information access easier

Once you've established what information different departments or groups within your organization want to access, work to improve the efficiency and accessibility of that information and associated resources.

The higher the barriers are between your people and the information they need, the less likely they are to try to get to the information. The barriers are a lot more than simple things such as intranet navigation and how searchable the content is. They also include things format: PDF, video, audio and how the information is presented (font size, paragraph length and layout, for example).

Every piece of information should be assessed for ease of access by the people who will need it. Scientific information for an R&D department will therefore need to be presented differently from basic machine tool procedures for a factory floor worker.

Writing for the computer screen

If, by now, you are considering various computer-based means of enhancing the informal learning capacity of your organization, you need to make sure you get this right from the start.

Almost all the material we consume these days is on a screen. How that material is presented is critical; it is very important that it is readily accessible. If the material is text, especially longer text pieces, there is an art to writing for the screen so that what is written has a high readability and comprehension level. The way material is written can be a massive barrier to readers, and here's why.

"It's life, Jim, but not as we know it." All Star Trek aficionados remember the immortal words of Mr Spock as he and Captain Kirk cast their sensors over some swirling mass of energy. We encounter a similar phenomenon every time we sit at a computer and type away. We are writing, and it is close enough to the writing we have done for centuries to seduce us into thinking the same golden rules apply. But they don't!

Compared with writing on stone, papyrus, vellum or paper, effective writing for the computer screen is radically different. Everything has changed and this can often lead to ineffective messages that are a waste of everyone's time.

Actually, the problem is not so much the writing, as the reading. We don't read on-screen text in the same way we approach the printed word. We are flooded with information on our screens, and we tend to train ourselves to cope with this, particularly when we are reading web pages. Eye-tracking studies of people reading web pages show that they skim fast and alight on words or phrases that literally catch their eye. The predominant pattern is also to spend more time around the top of the page and less at the bottom, and more on the left than the right.

One reason for the speed with which we skim screen information is because there is so much of it to get through. Another is because it is less comfortable to read from the screen. We tire at least 30 per cent faster when reading from the screen than from the page. How often have you printed out something in order to 'read it properly'? This is due to the relatively low screen resolution; text on a computer screen is less well-defined and not as accurately spaced as printed material. In addition, there is less contrast between the text and the background. We also have to cope with reflections and some older screens can be fuzzy and flicker. In time, the high resolution screens that are starting to become available on some high-end smartphones will solve these problems, but for now we are adapting our reading behaviour to cope.

Screen-adapted reading

How often have you had to follow up on an email in which you asked two questions, but only one was answered? Adaptation is the problem. Once we have altered our reading to deal with an internet overloaded with information, we carry that reading behaviour into everything we read on screen – emails, reports, letters, procedures manuals, blogs, wikis, specifications and so on. Unfortunately, most of these are not written with an understanding of how to write for the screen, and our adapted reading behaviour means that we miss important points.

People will take far less time to read on screen than you might hope. If the ideas are not easily and quickly accessible, the writing has failed because, on screen, people simply won't spend the time to unravel it.

You can read your own writing on screen perfectly well. You understand the flow, the ideas, the phraseology. Your reader does not. So as you proofread your emails or your blog post (you do proofread them, don't you?), your reading experience is not the same one your readers will have. They will have a much tougher time of it.

What you see on screen may well be quite different from what your reader sees. With the printed form, we have ultimate control over how it will look, apart from the amount of light available at the time it is read. With the screen, we have at best dual control, and we can be easily overridden by both the reader and the computer on which the piece is being read. The reader may have set preferences, automatically changing such things as font types, sizes and background colour. A common example is plain text versus formatted emails. The reader may have a different size screen from yours, or may be reading within a smaller window, so the text wraps in a different way.

Another issue is that on screen, there are so many distractions. These include buttons to click on, popups about incoming email or the latest stock quote, plus other windows that may be open, with programmes running ready to seduce your reader away at the slightest pretext. You seldom have their full attention in the first place, so losing them is easy; the difficulty is that when you are writing, you have no idea who else will be competing for your reader's attention. It is essential that what you write can be easily consumed and not trumped even by trivial distractions.

And strangely enough, we writers can even provide those distractions ourselves. Most writers adopt a carefree approach to writing on screen: we just let the words out because we know that it is so easy to go back and correct them, and there are spelling and grammar checkers to help us. The problem is, we often don't go back and check things properly, especially with shorter pieces. Our mind plays tricks on us so that when we get to the end, it is finished; it looks neat and tidy and it looks finished! And so we move on, leaving mistakes and simple errors in our wake – errors that can be so annoying that people feel less inclined to read our piece, while they also make judgements about our credibility and authority in the subject area.

So much potentially valuable information that is available on screen has much less influence and impact than it deserves due to its relative inaccessibility. It gets the back button treatment by people looking for information and input to informal learning.

We would do well to heed the words of Confucius as if they apply to our writing for the screen. "If language is not correct, then what is said is not what is meant; if what is said is not what is meant, then what ought to be done remains undone."

Chapter 10

Getting managers more involved

"Participants need to deliver more value to the business as a result of development, yet without line management involvement in the process, results are far from guaranteed."

Joanna Knight & Rob Sheppard

Line managers have a critical role to play in learning and development – that of supporting the development of their people. They are the link between L&D and the organization's business strategy.

Your biggest assets and also biggest liabilities, when changing skills and attitudes, are the managers of employees. Line managers need to be fully invested in any and all learning initiatives, as their support can make or break them.

They have a very large impact on how people learn on the job, and this impact often reflects the manager's own attitude towards learning. Spend time with the line managers and discuss how you can work with them to get the best from your L&D initiatives, whether these involve formal training or enhancing informal learning. After all, it is to the line managers' advantage in the long run.

Teach them about informal learning and the 70:20:10 ratio model. Explain how this is good news for them, as they are right there in the learners' everyday environment, so they are in an ideal position to influence the 70 per cent.

They should grab this opportunity with both hands and realize their impact on how, and what, people learn in the workplace.

Help them understand that the people in their team will always be learning, so they need to make sure they are learning the right things. If the system does not work well, then people will learn to bypass or ignore the system. If the required information is not readily available, people will learn how to cope without the right information. In both cases, the results will probably be substandard. So it is up to them to get the system right, so people learn the right ways to do things. And it's also up to the line managers (and L&D) to make sure the right information is readily available when it is needed, so people have the tools for doing the job well.

Getting line managers to coach rather than tell is crucial to helping them help their team members to learn and grow. One of your priorities may therefore be to develop coaching skills and to foster a coaching/mentoring culture within your learnscape.

Robin Hoyle, Head of Learning at Infinity Learning, says the line manager's role cannot be overestimated: "The ability to undertake self-learning is determined by workload and the priority given to competing tasks, which is determined by the line manager; it is the line manager who is responsible for creating the time and space for learning to happen."[130]

More often than not, however, they are not completely engaged in the training process. A CIPD study found that while more than 90 per cent of respondents believe line managers are 'important' or 'very important' in supporting L&D in their organization, only one in ten thought that line managers take learning and development very seriously.[131]

"At present, line managers are quite often playing no role in L&D," says Hoyle. "The issue is less whether they are supporting it than whether they are even allowing it."

Why are they so reluctant to be more involved in learning?

One reason is that people are often not natural coaches. Their natural inclination is to focus on the business and directly on the results and KPIs they are being measured against. Even if they have received coaching, this does not automatically equip them to deliver coaching. That's like saying people who have been to the top restaurant should be able to recreate the chef's signature dish.

What's more, the skills of a line manager are not necessarily the skills of the coach. While line managers are required to take a directive approach, coaching tends to use a non-directive approach, so that employees are encouraged to come up with their own solutions.

Typically, line managers receive very little training or development support to enhance their professional and leadership skills. Although they have a huge impact on how their direct reports learn on the job, very little is done in any formal way to improve their people management skills, and some of the most important of these are leadership, engagement and coaching skills.

People are often promoted into roles where they need to supervise and manage others, based on their technical or functional ability, and their organization then relies on whatever intrinsic talent they may or may not have for managing direct reports.

In their book, **The Talent Powered Organization**, Peter Cheese and his co-authors say the demands on line managers will increase as workforces become more diverse, virtual, have higher expectations and different attitudes to work and employment.[132]

"If workforce engagement today is in some state of decline, and we know that immediate line managers and supervisors are the most significant influences on engagement, and they also impact individual and team development, then we must put more in to supporting them and teaching them how to manage people in this new world," they say.

Consultants Joanna Knight and Rob Sheppard identified the following skills line managers perform to support development:[133]

- Listening
- Supporting
- Challenging
- Observing
- Motivating

- Setting objectives
- Providing business context
- Exploring mistakes
- Helping to focus effort
- Coaching
- Setting problems
- Providing opportunities
- Unblocking obstacles
- Encouraging risk taking
- Feedback
- Reinforcing.

Why don't they engage?

So why do so few line managers take learning and development seriously? There are various reasons, including a lack of time, awareness, desire, knowledge, ability or reinforcement.

Lack of time

A Cegos study found that managers feel they are far too busy.[134] The recession has exacerbated that situation. Line managers focus more than ever on the activities they and their senior managers regard as having the most immediate impact on the bottom line, such as winning new business, keeping customers happy and keeping the production line rolling. Most don't see training or people development as a core part of their role, so they don't set aside the time to do them.

Lack of awareness

Line managers are often unaware of the impact they have on their direct reports' development. They simply don't realize the role they play. They can also make it difficult for their direct reports to use new skills and fail to notice or recognize them when they do.

Lack of desire

Line managers may regard learning and development as something separate from running the business, rather than as a method of performance improvement. They don't see a direct correlation between development and better results, and so they rely on other methods, such as carrot and stick, to manage performance.

Lack of knowledge

Line managers may not know how to encourage development in their direct reports. For example, they might not realize that they need to follow up training or learning interventions. They almost certainly don't know about the 70:20:10 model and the implications that brings to their role.

Lack of ability

Line managers may not be able to translate their knowledge into supportive behaviour. They may lack support from L&D professionals and others within the organization to help them understand what learning is and how it takes place. They may need to learn skills such as coaching and mentoring.

Lack of reinforcement

Line managers might not be held to account for their support of development. This lack of 'measurement' might lead them to believe it is not important.

How to involve line managers

If any of the above is true of line managers in your organization, then you need to take action to change things.

Give them time

Line managers all too often say they are too busy to manage training or learning. L&D professionals need to focus their attention on the managers of those managers to ensure that learning becomes a priority within the organization, and that line managers are given time in their day. This will help develop a learning culture and ensure that learning is embedded from the top-down.

Focus on performance improvement not L&D

To convey how important learning and development is to the business and its employees, L&D professionals must be able to talk the same language as line managers. To really engage line managers' interest, focus on improving capability and thus performance, and how it relates to business measures rather than learning and development.

Get the business to own it

Begin by building connections and defining the need for learning and development with the business. Start embedding learning as a core value within the business. Educate the business about the value and benefits of learning and its impact on the bottom line and long-term growth.

Get the business to deliver/co-deliver it

Use line managers to deliver or co-deliver to their teams and to other staff. This, of course, includes all kinds of learning interventions, from the casual encouraging remark right through to a classroom situation.

Seek feedback from line managers

Line managers have a vital role to play in providing feedback on how successful different training and learning initiatives are, so get their views. What's more, they are the people who can ensure that what is learned is implemented and practised in the day-to-day working environment.

This knowledge needs to be shared with the L&D department. Even though the organization might have a process for obtaining feedback on the application of learning and its business impact, informal conversations with line managers will reveal important insights that will help you refine the end-to-end learning process and better understand your participants' needs within the business context.

Further development requirements which need to be addressed if performance is to be improved might be revealed in conversations.

Maintain momentum

Continue to engage with line managers to keep them focused and up-to-date through online manager communities, newsletters, updates, tips and text messages.

Accountability

Hold line managers to account for supporting the development of their people. If senior leaders are seen to contribute to development programmes, they will send out a strong message that development is important and other managers will follow their lead.

Develop learning champions

Develop champions for learning across the organization, from the top-down. The more positive and productive a learning experience a line manager has, the more likely it is that they will become a champion of learning. Managers who positively support the development of their team tend to be actively involved in learning. Those who are only focused on the task tend to be less supportive of training and learning and other aspects of people development.

Define the need

Line managers often don't have a clear definition of exactly what is expected of them in terms of developing their people. While their job profile might include something like 'manage the team effectively to deliver its objectives', it won't define what this means in terms of actions and behaviours, and specifically how these relate to training and learning.

Make sure training and learning is incorporated into job descriptions and performance objectives.

Communicate regularly

It's imperative that L&D communicates with line managers regularly to encourage their involvement in training and learning.

Take time to talk with line managers about the business drivers and specific challenges they face, and find out how L&D initiatives can be better aligned to their individual goals and those of the business. You will find this is time well spent.

Help line managers to understand staff needs

Line managers don't often understand their direct reports and how their skills can be improved, so it's vital that L&D professionals help them. They should also be encouraged to think more about the trends and behaviours they are seeing in people and how their skills can be better developed.

Involve line managers more in the coaching of employees, and using performance management systems and talent management methodologies.

Knowledge retention

For learning to have an impact, line managers need help in connecting the dots. They must see the importance of putting an action plan together with the employee, after the initial learning initiative or training course has ended. L&D professionals can help with this process.

Give them options

Let line managers know about the very latest information on available learning and training methods, programmes, tools and opportunities. All too often, line managers replicate their own learning experiences, which were probably rooted in traditional approaches.

Help them understand the importance of informal learning and the implications of the learnscape; then get them involved in improving it.

Chapter 11

Evaluating informal learning

"Everything that can be counted does not necessarily count; everything that counts cannot necessarily be counted."

Albert Einstein

It's understandable that organizations want to know if and how informal learning affects performance and business goals.

Typically, L&D professionals evaluate learning programmes as a way of assessing their effectiveness, to determine whether learning occurred and to demonstrate accountability. Evaluation involves demonstrating a return on investment (ROI), which shows not only that the learners have mastered the skills and knowledge presented in the training programmes, but also that, in their doing so, the organization has realized a benefit that exceeds the cost of the training programme.

With formal learning, it's possible to measure learning products and their effectiveness. The learning programme is well defined and finite, and the measures can be set against objectives. The two most prominent evaluation approaches are Kirkpatrick's 4 Levels of Evaluation and Phillips's ROI Methodology. Both assess attitudes about training, knowledge and skill acquisition, application of learning and performance improvement.

Measuring informal learning using those approaches presents difficulties. For a start, learners quite often follow their own objectives (which are not always aligned with those of the organization); also, the source of the learning is vast and the learning is infinite (there is no discernible end to it).

Saul Carliner, author of *Informal Learning Basics*,[135] gives the following reason (just one of several) on why Kirkpatrick's evaluation does not work with informal learning. Nearly all informal learning programmes are designed at least in part by the employees themselves for their unique needs at the time. If employees are asked to assess their reactions to the informal learning event, as per Kirkpatrick, they will be evaluating their satisfaction with their own customized, one-use only learning programme. "Assuming the worker was even aware that learning happened at all," adds Carliner.

These differences in the nature of formal and informal learning result in different issues driving evaluation, he says. "While measuring learning and its impact drives evaluation of formal learning, merely figuring out whether people learned anything at all and what they learned often drives the evaluation of informal learning."

But just because informal learning can't be measured in the same way as formal learning, this doesn't mean it should not be measured. If it's done well, measurement can determine whether the organization's investment in informal learning should increase or not. It can also determine whether to invest in technology tools or more personalized initiatives.

Companies that support and fund informal learning enablers might invest in electronic performance support systems, launch communities of practice, and develop, resource, manage and maintain knowledge bases. Given the investment required to facilitate, promote and enable informal learning, they're certain to want to know what they're getting in return.

Research by Knowledge Advisors, a leading provider of learning and talent management solutions, revealed that organizations that systematically measure their informal learning have budgets that are twice that of their counterparts that do not measure. Measure the informal learning, suggests the company in a white paper, and it becomes more visible and strategic and more budget is allocated its way.[136]

One way to measure informal learning is to look at three key elements: what to measure, when to measure and how to measure it, according to Knowledge Advisors.

What to measure

Organizations should measure informal learning based on the following three constructs: solution, experience and benefit.

The solution construct is measuring the informal learning to answer the question "Is this the right delivery type to fulfil the stated need?" It measures whether or not it was easy to access and use and whether it met the objectives. The key components of the solution construct include its availability/accessibility, whether it fulfilled objectives, and its effectiveness and usability.

The experience construct answers the question "Did the informal learning have the right level of community and involvement?" The key components of the experience construct include the learning's value, quality and engagement, and whether it was the right solution for the learning needed.

The benefits construct answers the question "Did the informal learning meet or exceed individual and organizational measurable performance goals and outcomes?" The key components of the benefits construct include the business results/return on investment, performance impact, application to the job, and its impact on the learner's professional growth.

Informal learning resources should be measured with the additional constructs: usability, user readiness, and enhanced community.[137]

- Usability: is the technology or new process usable and effective for its intended purpose?
- User readiness: how ready is the learning community to embrace this way of learning?
- Enhanced community: has the investment enabled meaningful connections between employees, increased engagement and provided value to them?

These measurements will reveal what is working or not and why it is working or not.

When to measure it

After knowing what to measure, a logical question to ask is when to measure it. John Mattox, Director of Research at Knowledge Advisors, says the ideal moment to measure is at the point of need, right when the learning is occurring.[138] In the desktop environment, measurement is feasible at that moment, using brief surveys, typically micro-polls or pop-up surveys.

Timing is more challenging for person-to-person events. Evaluation tools can be deployed for community events, either by paper, at the event, or electronically, after the event. Evaluating person-to-person events is rarely aligned to a consistent moment of need, but those moments still can be measured in a timely manner, says Mattox.

For coaching and mentoring programmes, an evaluation can be sent on a regular basis – quarterly, say, or twice a year – to check in on the process and its effectiveness.

Similarly, on-the-job experience can be evaluated at set intervals, such as after the first 90 days or bi-annually.

How to measure it

The measurement time should be proportionate to the time spent on the learning, says Mattox. Because informal learning requires measuring different constructs at different points in the process, you will need multiple measurement methods to do the actual measurement. Focus groups, interviews and observation, for example, can help measure the solution's usability and effectiveness.

At each interaction, a quick poll of the user, in the form of a feedback link or content rating, is a way to gauge the solution. Taking a sample of participants and conducting a more formal survey or assessment at the periodic milestone is effective in measuring the experience (and, of course, surveys and assessments also offer practical ways to measure benefits).

It doesn't make sense for a learner who has logged into a knowledge portal to look for a document to then be sent an evaluation document with 20 questions about their knowledge acquisition, performance improvement and how the learning will be applied on the job. But it does make sense for the learner to be asked, via a micro-poll or survey, a few questions, such as:

- Did you find what you need?
- If yes, was it easy to find?
- If no, what are you looking for?

"Such simple questions help assess whether the content is relevant for users," says Mattox.

With other types of informal learning, such as mentoring and coaching, more lengthy evaluation tools can be developed and deployed on a regular basis, because they do not interrupt the learning moment.

The survey should still be brief and aligned with the needs of the informal event. For example:

- Do you have a coach or mentor? (Y/N)
- On a scale of one to five, to what extent are you gaining value for your career growth from the coaching or mentoring sessions?
- What are the most valuable aspects of the sessions?
- What are the least valuable aspects?
- How can the session be improved?

The end of coaching and mentoring initiatives provides good opportunities for L&D to gather information from participants. As well as survey measures, organizations can also use key person interviews, focus groups or existing measurement tools.

For web portals and communities of practice, it is particularly useful to gather web analytics from a content management system or Google Analytics, stating how long people remain on a site, which links are followed, how often they visit, and whether they contribute to the site.

Other statistics are provided through social networking. When organizations use private social networking software, they can track the use of those networks.

The type of information provided through analytics includes:

- The number of uses – the number of times the online material was accessed and which pages were most popular
- The number of unique users, which identifies the number of people who visited a page, and whether a particular person visited the page one or 100 times; this reveals whether single users visited several times or users typically visit a page just once
- How long people stayed on the webpage – the length of time an individual stays on a website or webpage may indicate that he or she is engaged with the content.

Analytics can't explain why people choose to use certain resources and not others, or their level of satisfaction with the resources. To get that, you need to use analytics as well as looking at the individual's skills assessment, certifications as a result of informal learning, and notes from coaching sessions.

Measuring capability

Of course, measuring What, When and How for informal learning still misses a fundamental point. Why are we concerned about informal learning? Because it is a route to employees being capable in the moment when confronted with a task. Our desired end result of improving informal learning is the presence of capability in the moment when it is needed.

If people step up to a task and are capable, then the task will be done well. If not, chances are it will not be done well. So perhaps we should be measuring how well people are doing their tasks, as this is a measure of capability.

In many organizations, errors are tracked using either in-process measures or end of process measures because errors are costly in terms of rework or customer complaints. These same error rates are an indicator of the capability of the employees (and also a measure of the capability of the systems and 'machinery' the employee is utilising). Many times employees are shipped off to 'remedial' training courses to try to reduce the error rate, but it is often not a problem that off-the-job training can solve. Attention to on-the-job informal learning methods can be more effective and cost less to implement, improving capability and bringing the error rates down.

Ultimately it is about capability.

Conclusion

"The illiterate of the 21st century will not be those who cannot read and write, but those who cannot learn, unlearn, and relearn."

Alvin Toffler

The changes in today's knowledge-based, global economy are redefining the terms and conditions of work, its content and the context in which it takes place. It is now more complex, unpredictable, interconnected and virtual.

This means employees must be adaptable, responsible, multi-dimensional in problem solving, continuous learners, innovative, and willing to share what they know with their colleagues. They must rapidly acquire and successfully apply vast amounts of new information in response to constantly-changing technology and work conditions, which means the ability to continuously learn is among the most important and necessary of these skills.

To achieve that, they need to work in an environment that recognizes the need for learning and so provides every possible opportunity for them to find information, learn from it and then share it.

They learn most of what they do on-the-job informally, whether that's via an instant message, an email, a chat room session, a scheduled web-based meeting, a conversation with a colleague, coach or mentor, or even a chance encounter with a colleague. That's the way they like to learn.

Employers and L&D professionals have long talked about the value of their most important asset – people – and now, more than ever, they must do what they can to develop, enhance, engage and retain that asset.

As you've discovered, informal learning provides a way to improve employee capability and organizational performance. Equally importantly, it can be a critical element in employee engagement, and hence retention. Investing time and resources in people, learning resources and information technology can directly impact company results. All of which gives L&D a mission-critical role to play in the leadership success stories of the future.

One way L&D can achieve this is by creating or enhancing the collaborative learning environments. Getting started doesn't have to be an organization-wide project, but a step-by-step process involving one team at a time.

The case studies and examples in this book show that the results will be more than worth it.

I hope you have found this book useful and above all thought-provoking. Did you scribble notes in the margins next to ideas you can use in your workplace? I hope so; because above all my wish is that you take some of what you have encountered in this book and make use of it.

Don't leave the ideas lingering in the book stuck on the bookshelf. Take them out for spin and notice what results you get when you start doing things a little differently.

My best wishes,

Paul

Paul Matthews

P.S. You are welcome to drop me a line if you have any comments or suggestions. My email address is paul.matthews@peoplealchemy.com

www.peoplealchemy.com

About the author

Paul's life and work history can only be described as a little unusual.

He grew up on a hill country farm in New Zealand and went on to study both Agriculture and Engineering at University. He graduated with first class honours and a couple of years later won a national farm machinery award for the design of a seed drill. The drills were exported by his employer to over 20 countries around the world. Years later, when he was travelling in Ecuador, he was amazed to see one of his seed drills up for sale in a second-hand farm machinery yard by the side of the road.

As many Kiwis do, he set off to see the world and travelled extensively, stopping along the way to earn money for the next adventure. He then landed what was to him a dream job, working for an adventure travel company leading overland expeditions into many remote areas of the world. All this experience, which lasted over four years, has given him some great stories to tell of far-flung places, from the Congo jungle to the Chinese Taklamakan desert. By the way, locals say the name means 'go in and you will never come out'.

Paul then 'got a real job' as an engineer in the UK. It proved quite a challenge to make the transition from travelling the wild places on the planet and needing to build a campfire each night, to working regular hours and commuting.

After some success, he was headhunted into a NASDAQ-quoted multi-national technology company, where he eventually held the role of Customer Services Director. It was during this time that he really started to appreciate the importance of learning, and was surprised that his adventures and the experience of observing people learn to cope with unfamiliar situations were so valuable in understanding learning. His curiosity led him into studying psychology, NLP and many other areas relating to how the mind works – knowledge which he could then translate back into the workplace.

The constraints of corporate life lost their appeal and Paul started his own company, People Alchemy Ltd, in 1999, working as a consultant, trainer and coach in the areas of management and leadership. Most of his clients were blue chip organizations and one client programme had over 1,200 delegates.

He soon recognized the need for more direct performance support and the importance of informal learning in all its guises, rather than the common L&D reliance on classroom training. Paul has a way of engaging people with this changing paradigm so they can grasp it, incorporating it into their own organizational learning and capability strategies. His approach helps people to fully cater to the learning needs of their staff so they can get the job done.

References

1 C. R. Rogers, *Freedom to Learn*, Columbus, OH: Charles Merrill, 1983
2 D. Leonard and D. Kiron, 'Managing Knowledge and Learning at NASA and the Jet Propulsion Laboratory', *Harvard Business Review*, October 29, 2002
3 J. Cross, *Informal learning: Rediscovering the Natural Pathways That Inspire Innovation and Performance*, Pfeiffer, John Wiley & Sons, 2007
4 P. Senge, *The Fifth Discipline*, Random House, 1990
5 B. Mosh, Global Chief Learning and Strategy Evangelist, LearningGuideSolutions.com
6 'Learning to Change report 2010', Capita Learning & Development, www.capitald.co.uk, 2010
7 'McKinsey Global Survey 2010', McKinsey & Company, www.mckinseyquarterly.com, 2010
8 Corporate Leadership Council Survey 2011', Corporate Leadership Council, https://clc.executiveboard.com, 2011
9 'Internet Time Alliance Survey of CLOs 2009', www.internettimealliance.com, 2009.
10 'Learning and Talent Development 2012', Chartered Institute of Personnel and Development/Cornerstone OnDemand, www.cipd.co.uk
11 P. Weaver, S. Mitchell, 'Lessons for Leaders from the People Who Matter: How Employees Around the World View Their Leaders', Development Dimensions International, Inc., 2011
12 Orion Partners, 'UK Workers Say Only 1 in 20 Bosses Are Good Leaders', www.orion-partners.com, 2012
13 'Driving Performance and Retention Through Employee Engagement', Corporate Leadership Council, Corporate Executive Board, 2004
14 E. Davidove (Ph.D.), P. Butler 'The business case for social learning: dealing with the "capability recession" at lower cost', www.accenture.com, April, 2009

15 A. Pickerden, 'The extent to which informal learning is a neglected dimension of learning at work', ECLO 2004

16 J. Clemmer, 'Why Most Training Fails', The Clemmer Group, www.jimclemmer.com

17 P. Cheese, R. J. Thomas, E. Craig, *The Talent Powered Organization: Strategies for Globalization, Talent Management and High Performance*, Kogan Page, 2008

18 'Talent Edge 2020: Blueprints for the New Normal', Deloitte, December, 2010

19 'The 2009 State of Industry Report', ASTD Research, www.astd.org, 2009

20 J. Hagel III, J. Seely Brown, L. Davison, *The Power of Pull – How Small Moves Smartly Made Can Set Big Things in Motion*, Basic Books, Perseus Books Group, 2010

21 S. Herring, 'Transforming the Workplace – Critical Skills and Learning Methods for the Successful 21st Century Worker', Intrepid Learning, www.intrepidlearning.com

22 Bersin & Associates, High Impact Learning Culture Study, 2010

23 ASTD, Tapping the Potential of Informal Learning, 2008

24 D. Leonard, D. Kiron, 'Managing Knowledge and Learning at NASA and the Jet Propulsion Laboratory', *Harvard Business Review*, October 29, 2002

25 V. Powers, 'Out of this world success: NASA's portal draws unprecedented crowds', *KM World* magazine, October 1, 2004

26 G. A. Wright, 'Agile Learning: Thriving in the New Normal', *Chief Learning Officer* magazine, Clomedia, December 26, 2009

27 D. L. Coutu, 'The Anxiety of Learning', *Harvard Business Review,* March, 2002

28 A. Rogers, *What is the Difference? A new critique of adult learning and teaching*, Leicester: NIACE, 2003

29 'Capturing Untapped Business Value Through Informal Learning', Saba, www.saba.com, 2008

30 J. Hagel, J. Seely Brown, 'From Push to Pull – Emerging Models for Mobilizing Resources', Working Paper, October, 2005

31 N. Milton, '8 demand side KM principles', Knoco stories, www.nickmilton.com

32 B. Jensen, J. Klein, 'Blind Spots', *Chief Learning Officer* magazine, Clomedia, April 27, 2011

33 D. Boutilier, "Work Around' or 'Jerk Around'? Social Injustice and the Creation of Information and Misinformation in the Ontario

Public Service' in *The Future of Lifelong Learning and Work: Critical Perspectives*, D.W.Livingstone, K. Mirchandani, P. H. Sawchuk (eds), Sense Publishers., 2008

34 Forrester Research, www.forrester.com, 2011

35 'Learning At Work: Workplace Appraisal Of Informal Learning', Centre for Education and Work, Winnipeg, Manitoba, July, 2004

36 A. Tough, Paper presented at the 3rd New Approaches to Lifelong Learning (NALL) Conference, University of Toronto: Ontario Institute for Studies in Education, Toronto, Canada

37 J. Cross, *Informal learning: Rediscovering the Natural Pathways That Inspire Innovation and Performance*, Pfeiffer, John Wiley & Sons, 2007

38 'The Teaching Firm: Where Productive Work and learning Converge', Center for Workforce Development Education Development Center, Inc. January 1998

39 'The Teaching Firm. Where Productive Work and learning Converge', Center for Workforce Development Education Development Center, Inc. January 1998

40 A. Tough, 'The Iceberg of Informal Adult Learning', Originally published as NALL Working Paper #08-1999,"Reflections on the Study of Adult Learning: A brief talk at the 3rd New Approaches to Lifelong Learning (NALL) Conference, Ontario Institute for Studies in Education of the University of Toronto," February 19, 1999, NALL, Toronto

41 P. R. Penland, 'Self-planned learning in America', University of Pittsburgh, 1977

42 G. Cheetham, G. Chivers, 'How professionals learn in practice: an investigation of informal learning amongst people working in professions', *Journal of European Industrial Training*, Vol. 25, Issue: 5, 2001

43 V. Marsick, K. Watkins, 'Informal and Incidental Learning. New Directions for Adult and Continuing Education', 89, 25-34, 2001

44 Peters, '2003 Canadian Adult Education and Training Survey', 2004; K. Kim, M. Collins Hagedorn, J. Williamson, C. Chapman, 'Participation in adult education and lifelong learning: 2000–01', Washington, DC: U.S. Department of Education, National Center for Education Statistics, 2004

45 M. Dale, J. Bell, *Informal Learning in the Workplace*, Volume 134 of Research Report Series, Great Britain, Department for Education and Employment, 2000

46 V. Belliveau, Cornerstone OnDemand, www.cornerstoneondemand.com

47 R. Sheppard, J. Knight, 'Delivering Value Through Development', *Training Journal*, June, 2011

48 B. Hoffman, '*Informal Learning: Tips, Tools and Intelligence for Trainers*', ASTD, 2005

49 J. Gold, R. Thorpe, A. Munford (eds), *Gower Handbook of Leadership and Management Development*, 5th edition, Gower Publishing Ltd, 2010

50 'The Teaching Firm: Where Productive Work and learning Converge', Center for Workforce Development Education Development Center, Inc. January 1998

51 A. Howard, D. P. Hughes, 'Learning and Development Outlook 2009: Learning in Tough Times', The Conference Board of Canada. 'Learning and Development: The Skills-Training Disconnect', Michael. Bloom, *Inside Edge* e-magazine, *Conference Board of Canada,* August, 2009

52 J. Cross, *Informal learning: Rediscovering the Natural Pathways That Inspire Innovation and Performance*, Pfeiffer, John Wiley & Sons, 2007

53 D. Livingstone, S. Stowe, 'Work time and learning activities of the continuously employed: A longitudinal analysis, 1998-2004', *Journal of Workplace Learning*, Vol. 19, No 1, 2007, Emerald Group Publishing Ltd, 2007

54 A. Nancherla, 'Knowledge Delivered In Any Other Form Is... Perhaps Sweeter', *T + D* magazine (ASTD), May, 2008

55 M. Chui et al, 'The social economy: Unlocking value and productivity through social technologies', www.mckinsey.com, July 2012

56 C. Schooley, 'Informal Methods Challenge Corporate Learning', Forrester Research

57 S. Carliner, *Informal Learning Basics*, ASTD Press, 2012

58 B. Jensen, J. Klein, *Hacking Work: Breaking Stupid Rules for Smart Results*, Portfolio Penguin, 2010

59 W. Chadwick, 'Ringing in the changes', *Training Journal*, February, 2012

60 'Mobile learning in the workplace – a cost-effective approach to improving learning retention', (www.iriss.org.uk) June 2012

61 K. Oakes, 'LCMS, LMS--They're not just acronyms but powerful systems for learning', *T & D* magazine, March, 2002

62 J. Hagel, J. Seely Brown, 'From Push to Pull – Emerging Models for Mobilizing Resources', Working Paper, October, 2005

63 J. H. Dyer, N. W. Hatch, 'Using Supplier Networks to Learn Faster', *MIT Sloan Management Review*, Spring, 2004

64 K. Ichijo, F. Kohlbacher, 'Tapping tacit local knowledge in emerging markets – the Toyota way', Knowledge Management Research & Practice, 2008

65 Federal Computer Week Custom Report ,
    www.fcw.com/informationsharing

66 Federal Computer Week Custom Report ,
    www.fcw.com/informationsharing

67 H. Havenstein, 'CIA, Pfizer, Wachovia and Sony execs suggest options
    for adopting Web 2.0', *Computerworld*, June 11, 2008

68 C. Tuutti, '3 tips to make the most of wikis', *Federal Computer Week*,
    July 13, 2012

69 'Intellipedia' – Wikipedia, the free encyclopedia. Retrieved from
    http.//en.wikipedia.org/wiki/Intellipedia

70 'Social media drives sharing', *Government Computer News*, Retrieved
    from http://en.wikipedia.org/wiki/Intellipedia

71 'Social media drives sharing', *Government Computer News*, Retrieved
    from http://en.wikipedia.org/wiki/Intellipedia

72 J. Bersin,'Formalized Informal Learning: A New Architecture for
    Corporate Training', Bersin & Associates, 2010

73 C. Hubert, B. Newhouse, W. Vestal, 'Building and Sustaining Communities
    of Practice in Next-Generation Knowledge Management: Enabling Business
    Processes', American Productivity Centre, Houston, 2001

74 B. La Porte, 'Knowledge is currency at the World Bank', *KM Review*, 2002

75 N. W. Foote, E. Matson, N. Rudd, 'Managing the knowledge manager',
    The McKinsey Quarterly, McKinsey & Company, August, 2001

76 'Supporting performance at Dixons Retail – integrating formal and
    informal learning', Case study by Towards Maturity, March, 2012

77 B. Bain, 'YouTube for the intell community', *Federal Computer Week*,
    March 14, 2008

78 I. Nonaka, 'Strategy as Distributed Phronesis: Knowledge Creation
    for the Common Good', Hitotsubashi University Graduate School
    of International Corporate Strategy; 'Knowledge Management: From
    Brain to Business', International Productivity Conference 2007, Asian
    Productivity Organization 2007

79 S. Cantrell, N. Di Paolo Foster, 'Techniques for Managing a Workforce
    of One: Flexible Policies', Research Note, Issue 7, Accenture, 2007

80 J. Bersin,'Formalized Informal Learning: A New Architecture for
    Corporate Training', Bersin & Associates, 2010

81 M. McGuinness, 'An Introduction to Business Coaching',
    www.wishfulthinking.co.uk

82 S. Cantrell, N. Di Paolo Foster, 'Techniques for Managing a Workforce
    of One: Flexible Policies', Research Note, Issue 7, Accenture, 2007

83 M. Rose, 'Social Learning for a Social Workplace', Knoodle, www.enterprisecollaborative.com, November 16, 2011

84 D. Smith, S. Cantrell, 'Make Every Person Count: Customizing Talent Management', *Talent Management Magazine,* April, 2008

85 www.mcdonalds.com

86 S. Cantrell, N. Di Paolo Foster, 'Techniques for Managing a Workforce of One: Flexible Policies', Research Note, Issue 7, Accenture, 2007

87 www.flashmentoring.com

88 E. Wagner, 'Informal learning: Extending the impact of enterprise ideas and information', Adobe Systems Inc., 2007

89 J. Cross, *Informal learning: Rediscovering the Natural Pathways That Inspire Innovation and Performance*, Pfeiffer, John Wiley & Sons, 2007

90 R. Millar, 'It adds up: How accountants use Yammer', Diary of an internal communicator blog (www.rachmillar.com), June 23, 2012

91 www.mcdonalds.com

92 W. J. Rothwell, J. E. Lindholm, W. G. Wallick, *What CEOs expect from corporate training : building workplace learning and performance initiatives that advance organizational goals*, American Management Association, 2003

93 K. H. Silber, L. Kearny, *Organizational Intelligence: A Guide to Understanding the business of your organization for HR, training and performance consulting*, John Wiley & Sons, 2010

94 T. Jeary, T. Bingham, *Presenting learning: Ensure CEOs Get the Value of Learning*, ASTD, 2007

95 'McKinsey Global Survey 2010', McKinsey & Company, www.mckinseyquarterly.com, 2010

96 M. Harrison, '13 Ways of Managing Informal Learning', Kineo, 2006

97 McKinsey Global Survey of Business Executives, July, 2005

98 R. L. Cross, R. D. Martin, L. M. Weiss, 'Mapping the value of employee collaboration', *The McKinsey Quarterly*, McKinsey & Company, No 3, 2006

99 R. Cross, A. Parker, 'The Hidden Power of Social Networks: Understanding How Work Really Gets Done', *Harvard Business Review*, 2004

100 V. Krebs, J. Holley, 'Building Sustainable Communities through Network Building', Valdis Krebs, 2002

101 R. L. Cross, R. D. Martin, L. M. Weiss, 'Mapping the value of employee collaboration', *The McKinsey Quarterly*, McKinsey & Company, No 3, 2006

102 Jay Cross, 'Bring Informal Learning Up to Date', www.jaycross.com, May 28, 2012

103 'Global Leadership Forecast 2011', DDI, 2011

104 'Employee Engagement Report 2011', Blessing White, Inc., December, 2010

105 '2010 Gallup Engagement Survey', 2010

106 'Becoming an employer of choice', CIPD

107 APCO Worldwide and Gagen MacDonald, Survey on the State of the U.S. Workplace as Viewed by America's Workforce, October 2011

108 D. MacLeod, N. Clarke, 'Engaging for success: enhancing performance through employee engagement', Department for Business, Innovation and Skills, Crown Copyright. July, 2009

109 J. Blain, 'Current learning trends in Europe and the United States' whitepaper, Cegos International Partners Network, 2009

110 Q. Clark, 'Reconciling Formal and Informal', Learnlets blog, http://blog.learnlets.com, May 24, 2012

111 T. Kelly, 'Measuring Informal Learning: Encourage a Learning Culture & Track It', www.trainingindustry.com, March 31, 2009

112 A. Chan, 'Driving Informal Organizational Learning – Tools and Strategies', www.organizational-learning.com.au, 2011

113 J. Bersin,'Formalized Informal Learning: A New Architecture for Corporate Training', Bersin & Associates, 2010

114 D. Wilkins, 'Learner-Driven Content: The Next Wave in Development', *Chief Learning Officer* magazine, (Clomedia), April 29, 2008

115 C. Tuutti, '3 tips to make the most of wikis', www.fcw.com, July 2012

116 'Collaboration Tools' special report, Government Computer News, www.GCN.com/collaborationtools

117 J. Hart, 'Building A Social Learning Environment For Free Or At Low Cost', *Inside Learning Technologies* magazine, January, 2010

118 E. Davidove, P. Butler, 'The business case for social learning: Dealing with the "capability recession" at lower cost', Outlook (Accenture), April, 2009

119 N. Allen, T. Burgess, *CompanyCommand: Unleashing the Power of the Army Profession*, Center for the Advancement of Leader Development & Organizational Learning, 2001

120 N. Allen, T. Burgess, *Taking the Guidon: Exceptional Leadership at the Company Level*, The Center for Company-Level Leadership, 2001

121 R. Deiser, *Designing the Smart Organization, How Breakthrough Corporate Learning Initiatives Drive Strategic Change and Innovation*, Jossey-Bass, 2009

122 E. Davidore, C Mindrum, 'Verifying Virtual Value', *Chief Learning Officer* magazine, (Clomedia), February 28, 2010

123 N. W. Foote, E. Matson, N. Rudd, 'Managing the knowledge manager', *The McKinsey Quarterly*, McKinsey & Company, August, 2001

124 A. Chan, 'Driving Informal Organizational Learning – Tools and Strategies', www.organizational-learning.com.au, 2011

125 P. Kettley and W. Hirsh,' Learning from Cross-functional Teamwork', The Institute for Employment Studies, 2000

126 J. D. Sostrin, 'Establishing and validating a conceptual framework of barriers to workplace learning and performance: A Q-method study', 2008

127 D. L. Coutu, 'The Anxiety of Learning', *Harvard Business Review,* March, 2002

128 D. L. Coutu, 'The Anxiety of Learning', *Harvard Business Review,* March, 2002

129 J. Pfeffer, R. I. Sutton, *The Knowing Doing Gap: How Smart Companies Turn Knowledge Into Action*, Harvard Business School Press, 2000

130 H. Abbott, 'The bottom line', www.learningmagazine.co.uk

131 'Annual survey report 2007', Learning and Development, CIPD, 2007

132 P. Cheese, R. J. Thomas, E. Craig, *The Talent Powered Organization: Strategies for Globalization, Talent Management and High Performance*, Kogan Page, 2008

133 J. Knight, R. Sheppard, 'The role of line managers in L&D', *Training Journal*, September, 2011

134 'The Cegos checklist for getting line managers more involved in training', Cegos, www.cegos.co.uk

135 S. Carliner, *Informal Learning Basics*, ASTD Press, 2012

136 'Informal Learning Measurement', White Paper, Knowledge Advisors, www.knowledgeadvisors.com, 2010

137 P. Parsley, 'Formal Numbers for Informal Learning', *Chief Learning Office* magazine, Clomedia.com, October 25, 2009

138 J. R Mattox III, 'Measuring the Effectiveness of Informal Learning Methodologies', February 2012

Index